The
New Patient
Generator

The New Patient Generator

The Complete Guide to 20+ New Patients
Per Month for Healthcare Practitioners

Colin Swala

The New Patient Generator
The Complete Guide to 20+ New Patients Per Month for Healthcare Practitioners

Published by Rebel Press
Austin, TX
www.RebelPress.com

ISBN: 978-1-68102-941-2

Printed in Canada

This book is dedicated to everyone who has inspired me to shoot for the stars. To my mother Cheryl, from the beginning you always supported me in the pursuit of my dreams and never stood in the way. I know that your support continues from the other side. I miss you Mom and love you forever.

To my father Carl, you also left this world too soon but you're ambitious drive to achieve something great was left behind and I hope that this book will make you proud. I love you Dad and miss you too.

To my wife Katherine, the love of my life, my best friend and biggest supporter. The journey is long and hard so thank you for being strong and sticking with me through thick and thin. It seems at times there's more thick than thin but..... we're almost there.

And finally, to all the hardworking healthcare practitioners who's mission is to help as many people as possible find better health through their services and education. I hope this book will help you serve to maximum capacity and that even more people will get well as a result.

CONTENTS

INTRODUCTION... 1

- o   Oh, How Marketing Has Changed
- o   Marketing for Health?
- o   Reach, Downloads, Leads, Lists, New Patients, and Beyond
- o   Drinking Water from a Fire Hose

THE BIG WHY.. 9

- o   "Who the heck is this guy?"
- o   Through Challenge Comes Opportunity

HUNTING VERSUS FARMING.................................. 13
FUN-NEL FACTS 17

- o   The Marketing Funnel
- o   TOFU – MOFU – BOFU Vs. AIDA
- o   Customer Journey vs. Sales Funnel
- o   The Landing Page

The New Patient Generator Setup – Day 1 & 2 27

- o   Ready, Set, Go!
- o   What is a Blog?
- o   Choosing Your Platform
- o   Who Likes Traffic?
- O   Step 1: Topic Research
- O   Step 2: Choose Your Blog Platform
- O   Step 3: Choose 6 Of The Most Popular, Aggravating, Pressing Topics Or Pain Points That Your Ideal Patient Or Client Is Faced With – The Ones That You Have The Solution For.
- O   Step 4: Write Catchy Titles Your Audience Can't Resist

o Step 5: The Anatomy Of The Perfect Health Blog (It's Time To Get Writing!)
o Step 6: Publish Your Blogs

The New Patient Generator Setup – Day 3, 4 & 5 53

o Brace Yourself
o The Top 6 Social Media Platforms You Need for Your Practice
o Step 1: Ensure You Have Created The Correct Accounts For All The Social Platforms We've Discussed In This Chapter
o Step 2: Fully Complete Each Profile With As Much Information That You Would Like To Share About Yourself And Your Business
o Step 3: Source Your Twitter Chats And Existing Facebook Groups
o Step 4: Create Your Facebook Group(S)
o Step 5: Develop The Format For Your Practice Insta-Story Day Of The Week For Instagram
o Step 6: Create 6 Videos For Your Youtube Channel And Optimize For Search Engine Ranking
o Step 7: Create Content For Your Personal Facebook Profile, Practice Facebook Page, And Instagram And Load Your Scheduler
o Step 8: Organically Grow Your Following On Facebook

The New Patient Generator Setup – Day 6 91

o Integral to Digital Marketing
o Step 1 – Ensure You Have Set Up All The Information On Your Google Places For Business Account.
o Step 2 – Ask Your Current Patients Or Clients To Write A Review
o Step 3 – Set Up An Ongoing Bonus Structure For Your Staff For Each Review They Cultivate
o Step 4 – Reply To Your Reviews

The New Patient Generator Setup – Day 7, 8 & 9 95

- Email Marketing is Not Dead
- Email and the Prospective Patient/Client Journey
- Email Campaigns 365 – Automated/Triggered Emails vs. Scheduled/Manual Broadcasts
- Step 1: Choose Your Platform
- Step 2: Write Your Indoctrination And Engagement Campaigns And Set Up Email Automation
- Step 3: Set Up Your Email Automation
- Step 4: Map Your Holiday And Seasonal Promotions

The New Patient Generator Setup – Day 10, 11 & 12 ... 127

- Foundation of Digital Marketing
- 3 Types of Prospective Patients or Clients
- Anatomy of the Facebook Ad Campaign
- The Top 4 Facebook Ad Campaign Objectives for Health Care Providers
- Targeting
- Custom Audiences and Retargeting
- Split Testing
- The Other Social Platforms and Why Have I Left Them Out
- Step 1: Set Up Facebook Business Manager
- Step 2: Set Up A Facebook Pixel For Your Ad Account
- Step 3: Create Your Cold Audience Facebook Ads Campaign
- Step 4: Create Your Lead Magnet
- Step 5: Create Your Warm Audience Facebook Ads Campaign

The New Patient Generator Setup – Day 13 175

- Harnessing the Power of Google Ads
- Step 1: Ensure You Have A Google Adwords Account Setup
- Step 2: Determine Your Maximum Cost Per Click, Choose The Target Audience And Bid Option

    O   Step 3: Do Your Keyword Homework And Set Your Daily Budget

    O   Step 4: Create Your Ads

The New Patient Generator Setup – Day 14.................. 185

    o   Boring but Necessary
    o   Facebook Metrics
    o   Google AdWords Metrics
    o   Google Analytics Metrics
    o   Email Marketing Metrics
    O   Step 1: Set Up Your Google Analytics Account
    O   Step 2: Create Your Analytics Master Tracking Sheet

Epilogue 201

    o   Pop the Champagne!
    o   Maintenance on Your Machine
    o   Signing Off

The
New Patient
Generator

INTRODUCTION

*"Expect the Best, Prepare for The Worst,
Capitalize on What Comes." – Zig Ziglar*

By simply picking up this book, that tells me that you're a forward-thinker. Digital Marketing, also known as online marketing, is essential for any business whether you are running a small business or you run a multi-national corporation. If you don't learn how to do it yourself or hire an expert to manage it for you, then your business might not only be left in the dust, it might become dust! I think you know this already, which is why you're reading this.

This might sound extreme, but look at it this way. Marketing is only effective when you have an audience. If you put up a billboard in your living room, it won't reach anyone and therefore won't produce the desired result. You need a platform to get your message out to the masses while staying within the confines of the budget for your practice.

Oh, How Marketing Has Changed.

Throughout history, it's believed that the concept of marketing has progressed through five phases. In the early days there wasn't much to it. Marketing was simple because business was simple; most items were harvested by hand and traded. Then the industrial revolution hit which brought mass production and increased product availability. However, with limitations on competition there still wasn't much need for marketing. This lasted into the '40s where demand surged and competition increased. This sprouted the need for advertising, sales, and promotion, which traditionally was facilitated across three main platforms: print, radio, and TV. These three marketing platforms ruled initiatives for years with some disadvantages when compared to the platforms of today. They can be expensive and provide hardly any ability to target the customer. The core marketing platform available to the "little guy" was to pay for a listing in the yellow pages. And if they really stretched their budget, they could splurge for a larger sized ad and sit, wait, and pray that someone would stumble across their listing.

My father was about 5' 11" and close to 200 pounds yet, considered to be one of those "little guys" in business. He had business-building in his blood. His mother (my grandmother, Mary) left Ukraine in the early 1900s to find prosperity in Canada and landed in Toronto. She managed to achieve exactly what she sought. Grandma Mary built a very successful business in the hospitality industry. Through an unfortunate series of events that apparently was fueled by my Grandfather, my Grandmother lost her fortune and later passed away early while my estranged Grandfather left with her fortune and was nowhere to be found, leaving my father with nothing. What he did receive from the first perceived negative situation was a drive to build the family wealth once again. Although this was tough for my father, he was gifted with desire and drive to build his family wealth again one day.

My dad eventually met my mother who gave birth to his son, a blond haired, blue eyed beauty of a baby *cough*... me. Now at that point it was even more important to succeed so he started a courier business called Barrie Courier. The extent of his marketing initiatives was word-of-mouth and the good ol' yellow pages. Developing a successful business is hard. Without access to capital for investing in the large marketing platforms of the day, it would have made it even harder to succeed. Let's just say that his business did everything but thrive, although we survived and I'm here to tell the story.

However, "times they are a changing." With the rise of the internet and the now estimated 3.5 billion searches per day on Google, not to mention the other search engines and the over 3 billion users on social media platforms, the game has changed. Businesses of all sizes now have access to large audiences with what seems like endless capabilities to target customers/patients/clients at an affordable price. Therefore, I really believe that right now is the greatest time to be in business. Whether you own a brick and mortar style or developed an online marketplace for products or services, or whether it's a small single person operation or a massive 5000 employee monster, we all have access to one of the most powerful tools for exploding any business. But... there's a catch. You must know what you're doing.

To harness the power of current day digital marketing, you need to invest in one of two avenues. You will either invest your time to learn all pieces of the digital marketing puzzle like statistics tracking, paid and organic social media initiatives (Facebook, Twitter, YouTube, Pinterest, Instagram, LinkedIn, etc.), email marketing, and copywriting. Or you will invest financially into a marketing officer or agency who will do it for you. Since you're reading this book, then I'll assume that you fall in line with the former.

Marketing for Health?

Look over there... in the corner of your room... quick... there's an elephant! I've been marketing for the private healthcare industry for years now, reach millions of people per month with our client's marketing initiates, and have connected thousands of patients with doctors and private health practitioners all over the world. However, I'm writing to you from a country with a government-funded healthcare system, and being a former private healthcare professional myself, I've observed some challenges around the idea of marketing for healthcare practitioners. This might not be so apparent in other countries that only have private healthcare, but it might still apply.

"Why is a doctor advertising?" I've seen this comment from time to time on social media so I think it's important to address this question head-on so that you, the healthcare practitioner, can continue to market with confidence and assurance and so you have an answer for the more inquisitive members of your audience.

In many of the private health industries, there can be a disconnect between what the public perceives as what you CAN help with and what you DO help with. For example, I am a registered chiropractor and I know that part of the challenges limiting the growth of the profession is that the majority of the public have no idea to what extent we can help. So rather than taking the view that you are marketing your practice simply to fill your wallet, really what you're doing is helping shift the public perception of your profession while positioning yourself as a leader and helping more people in need, all while growing your business to help you expand to serve even more people. With this vision in mind, the public perception of your marketing initiatives will be positive.

Contrary, if your marketing campaigns are coming across as "salesy," money driven, and all about YOU (the practitioner) and how you will benefit, then the feedback will surely be negative and you won't be doing anything for the growth of your business or your profession.

Reach, Downloads, Leads, Lists, New Patients, and Beyond

When considering digital marketing for your practice, you're really looking to accomplish the following which is all covered in the chapters ahead:

- **Reach More in Your Community** – As a healthcare practitioner, you have a message for your community. You have tools to help them in ways they possibly don't even know. Your digital marketing initiatives will allow you to virtually stand on a milk crate in your town square and deliver that message to the masses. From this, you will consistently grow as the "go-to" health professional in your community. A leader in your profession.

- **Increase downloads** – Part of the process is to start building an online community. These people might not be members of your practice yet, but they are a very important extension in addition to being prospective patients down the road. To help build that community, you may produce educational pieces such as downloads or private-access videos to help showcase your knowledge and personality.

- **Build Your Email List Audience** – I once heard a digital marketer say it this way quite bluntly, "If you're not building an email list, you're an idiot." As insulting as that may sound (and I think he was half joking, which really means half-serious), he is right.
  - The number of e-mail users worldwide is forecasted to rise to 2.9 billion by 2019 – Statista
  - Nine in ten people surveyed told marketingsherpa.com they enjoyed getting emails from favored brands, so much so that 15 percent would be open to receiving them on a daily basis
  - Cost for developing long-term marketing campaigns

through email to your list is pennies when compared to paid sources.

o   More than three-quarters of consumers said they've made purchases influenced by emails – marketingsherpa.com

• **Generate Leads** – This is what results from a successful conversion. The ability to capture contact information for people in your community that have any interest in your service. This tee's up the opportunity to present low-cost offers to take the relationship offline and into your practice.

• **Maximize New Patients** – Being a health professional myself, I know there are many ways to produce new patients, and I would argue that the best patients are those that come from referrals. However, referrals have to come from current patients so you need a regularly flowing patient base to produce new referrals from. Once this new patient pipeline is automated and the stream is flowing, then you can focus on what you really enjoy the most – helping people.

We have been fortunate to help health practitioners at all stages of their journey. Take Jacob, he was a chiropractic student in the United States who was in his final year who found himself in a situation that may have prevented him from graduating (little side note, the same thing happened to me due to news of my mother's cancer in my final year so I know firsthand how stressful this situation can be). As you are probably aware, most health professional studies have a requirement for graduation that within the final year, you must see a set number of new patients and patient visits. With the end of the year closing in, Jacob found himself behind in his numbers. His finances, his pride, and maybe even his parents' unconditional love (harsh exaggeration but maybe true for some) was on the line. He contacted us in desperation (and nearly in tears) to help him connect with as many new patients in his area as possible before it was too late. Luckily for him and the many others we've helped in his situation, we like a good challenge, not to mention that we have a proven plan for healthcare practitioners that would produce exactly what he was looking for. Plus, we gave him a break on the cost because although we value every cent we charge, we love to help the next generation of healthcare providers get on their feet.

Considering the time constraint, we went ahead with a Facebook Lead Ads campaign with a video. We wrote a script for the video that leveraged the benefits for the patient of seeing him as a student, positioned himself ahead of the rest with all his past accomplishments and credentials, and created a clear Call-To-Action that would enable the prospective patients to jump on the opportunity. The result? Twenty-three new patient requests that month and a student who graduated successfully.

Drinking Water from a Fire Hose

This book is full of practical information organized into a step-by-step strategy by design. I've purposely left out much of the fluff. I recommend that you don't skip any of it when you start to implement. Although at a first glance, learning the material within two weeks might be like trying to drink from a fire hose and then attempting to build the machine and having it ready to turn on the ignition might seem like climbing Mount Everest, but I can assure you it's not only possible, it's simple when you have the plan. After you have completed Day 14 you will have created a new patient-generating machine that will passively drive 20+ new patients into your practice every single month.

This book has been organized by day so that you can build your engine step by step. By all means, if you work fast then you can work ahead or slow it down, but I wouldn't extend this process longer than a month because every day that goes by without this machine running, you are literally losing money, and patients are being left without answers to their health concerns. Once complete you just turn the key to "on" and sit back and watch the new patients roll in and your practice grow. I realize that some of you are at various places with your online marketing journey and are only looking for certain tips and tricks. If that is the case, then by all means, skip to the sections where you need help.

This is the only complete digital marketing strategy step-by-step guide for healthcare practitioners that I know of, and I promise that it will over deliver if you don't leave anything behind.

THE BIG WHY

"A Goal Is a Dream With A Deadline." – Napoleon Hill

"Who the Heck Is this Guy?"

Is that what you're thinking? Everyone is an online marketing expert these days so why should you listen to me? Great question. If you *are* thinking that, then you're just like me. I don't like to waste time or money, and if I'm going to invest either of those, then I want to be perfectly clear on who I let guide me.

My lengthy career journey started as a computer nerd. I fell in love with programming in high school and proceeded to college where I graduated in computer sciences. I loved it. I left college and went to work for an international communications company who manufactured nurse call systems where I managed the Canadian branch's website. During my time, I had the opportunity to develop a web-based media manager for educational facilities. This was exciting! My programming career was taking off. However, something was missing. Ever since my father passed away from a heart attack when I was only 15 years old, I had an itch for helping people improve their health that was not being scratched with the current path. Ironically at that moment, I was presented with a fork in the road. Chiropractic revealed itself, grabbed my arm, and lead me to a brand-new place. I knew right away that this was the missing link. Although I never took the computer nerd hat off, I started a 15-year journey of education

9

and health that would allow me to help thousands of people in my local community.

As a private practice health practitioner, helping people was the easy part. The business and the marketing were not. In college, we learned very little about business and marketing, yet it turns out that was a huge part of the job. I spent years learning how to market myself in practice but during that time the landscape changed. The internet presence in marketing was growing and the emergence of social media popularity started to change the game. Both my partners and I adapted all the best traditional marketing initiatives we could get our hands on. In-person health screenings, workshops, dinner with the doctor events, TV, radio, and print. Some were considered a "farming" approach and some were considered a "hunting" approach. I will explain more about these in the next chapter. They were all effective to some degree; however, some were time-consuming, limited, and quite expensive so they would be hard for ALL health practitioners to implement all the time. This problem eventually stumped me as well.

Through Challenge Comes Opportunity

In my final year in college, my mom called me and told me some terrible news. She just found out that she had cancer. I had already lost my father in my teenage years, so this news was really devastating for me. Fortunately, she fought a long hard battle and kept the fight going for 10 years. For most of that time you wouldn't even be able to tell how sick she was. However, in her final year, the disease started to really show its ugly head. Her ability to care for herself depleted, which meant my brother and I had to step up and care for her. This also meant that every second outside of the time I spent seeing patients was by her side. So now imagine what that meant for my practice. New patients were the lifeblood, and without any extra time, how was I going to survive a whole year! Luckily for me when I get pushed into a corner, beast mode switches on.

Even though I had to be near my mother every moment possible, I wasn't physically tied up the whole time. I had my laptop. I had my computer nerd hat. I had the solution to my current problem right under my nose. Digital marketing for my practice! What if I took what I learned prior with computers and fed on a buffet of digital marketing information that all the experts had to give or sell. This is exactly what I did. After implementing what I learned, the results blew my mind. This was too important to keep to myself, and therefore our digital marketing agency emerged.

Today we've collectively reached almost 15,000,000 people, connected thousands of new patients with health practitioners, and manage close to a million dollars per year in digital advertising budgets for our clients. Our success comes comes from the secrets that are revealed in this book. I have compiled everything I've learned along the way and wanted to share it so that your practice success will allow more people to find the answers to their health challenges and start their path to a better, happier life for them and their families.

One of the greatest thrills in working with health practitioners is hearing the stories of success from the people that we've worked with and who have implemented the elements of this system. Dr. Mark Del Cantero's story is one that stands out, which demonstrates that it's not just our clients and the people they serve that have had life-changing experiences after getting started. I was at a conference in Toronto, Canada recently that brought professional health practitioners together from all over North America. We had a booth to promote our services and were delighted to see familiar faces there, as many were already working with us. At these conferences the attendees are encouraged to bring their families, so both Mark and his wife Danielle popped by our booth to have a chat. Mark was thrilled and told me that since starting the service his practice has "blown up" through the number of new patients he receives and that the growth has been exponential due to family and friend referrals they receive from those patients. Mark is one of those guys with a huge heart. The kind of guy that you can feel his desire to serve his community to maximum capacity when you speak to him. It's so exciting that he is well on his way to seeing that through. Then his wife Danielle added another level that I hadn't thought about. She told me that she was thrilled with the service because the automation allowed her husband to de-stress, knowing there was going to be a consistent flow of new patients coming in. She said that this has positively affected the whole family. Now they are able to spend more time together on the weekend as Mark was able to give up time-consuming marketing events. She said it was just a "no brainer" for them to keep the new patient engine running.

I understand why some might shy away from learning all of this. At a first glance it looks like a mountain to climb, especially if they're not "techy." So fair enough; maybe they would just rather pay someone to do it all for them, which is why we also provide a done-for-you service. However, you *can* do it yourself, especially since I've filtered out all the digital marketing fluff, leaving a very concise, detailed plan of action catering specifically to healthcare practitioners.

HUNTING VERSUS FARMING

"Value the Relationship More Than the Quota." – Jeff Gitomer

I was at a media seminar in New Jersey that was organized for chiropractors specifically. There was a speaker who presented the marketing concept of farming versus hunting for new patients with regards to marketing online. I enjoyed that idea because it made perfect sense. Here is my description and interpretation:

Hunting: The idea of seeking out new patients or clients who might not otherwise know they need your service at that present time. Then deliver and present the information about yourself, your practice, and your profession and present an opportunity for them to take action. The health professional is taking the first step.

Farming: The idea of growing, building trust, or nurturing a relationship and then harvesting the new patient when the relationship has matured. Generally, the prospective patient or client is taking the first step.

The part that I disagreed with the speaker, however, is that it was presented that one was better than the other. In my opinion, a well-rounded marketing initiative would use both concepts to maximize success.

For example, for many private health professions, polls show that there is a larger number of people that don't know the extent of what you do or why they need what you have to offer. Therefore, simply building a website and hoping people in your community search you out for specific keywords will only help attract new patients or clients from a small pool of people. The same goes for organic traffic for your social media platforms like Facebook, Instagram, and YouTube, etc. If you are spending all your time or possibly your staff's time working on these, you will really be limiting yourself with your online marketing initiative. It's possible this is the preferred direction as it has the lowest upfront cost. If it produces a less than desirable result (which for most health practitioners I have spoken to, it has) then no harm no foul; we didn't lose very much and I guess marketing online doesn't really work. How wrong this is.

I consider the best approach to be one that includes both hunting and farming. Trust me, take the leap. A more than 10:1 return-on-investment (ROI) is waiting if you do.

Think about all you're trying to accomplish:

CALL
TO ➔

ACTION
BUTTON

- You want to give the opportunity to those people who didn't know there was a solution to their problem and want to jump on an opportunity to solve it right away

- You want to educate those who are blind to your profession and all it has to offer in order to turn on a light bulb in their head

- You want to place yourself in the right place at the right time when someone who knows how you can help wants to take action

- You want to hold the hands of skeptical people in your community and guide them through a journey where they end up in your practice

- You want to nurture your current patient community and empower them to share and refer

Marketing your practice online can be a numbers game. Don't restrict your success with limited thinking.

FUN-NEL FACTS

"If content is king, then conversion is queen." – John Munsell

The Marketing Funnel

Before we get into the nitty gritty, let's go over some more concepts that will help you wrap your head around what we're doing and why we're doing what we're doing. If you've even poked your head into the world of marketing at any point, you've probably heard the term "funnel." The terms purchase funnel, marketing funnel or sales funnel all refer to the same concept. In this book we will refer to the concept as the sales funnel, which by definition is an effective marketing process that leads customers through from a cold place where they don't know anything about your business or haven't thought of buying anything from you to being an actual customer.

For example, we have a client who is a personal trainer. He specializes in a rare form of exercise and is known as a leader for what he does. He wants to consistently fill a high-ticket price live certification platform through three stages. His challenge? To take personal trainers who don't know who he is and don't know anything about the exercise he teaches and have them pay a premium for his live certification course so they can run classes for the public and make lots of money doing it. How do we build the bridge for him to succeed? We develop a sales funnel online with all the resources he has available. We start by defining his ideal customer, which we know are personal trainers. Then we develop an awareness campaign to educate this group about our client, his credentials, his achievements, position him as the leader, explain the concepts of his new rare form of exercise, excite them by conveying how running classes have been extremely prosperous for him, and how it gives him the life of his dreams. Any interested PTs will click, watch, or share, which we pool into an audience of "interested" potential clients. Next up, move as many of these interested potential customers into a community for direct communication, which could be a private forum, private Facebook group, email list, etc. Through these interfaces, we create desire as the potential customer grows a stronger bond with our client, his brand, and/or his rare form of exercise. This sets the final stage of the sales funnel where the potential customer crosses over to initiate a purchase, starts a trial, or jumps in with both feet.

This framework is what is used in marketing offline and online. And whether the end goal is to have the customer/client/patient purchase a product, sign up for a certification course, or have a patient end up in your practice starting care, it's the same process.

TOFU MOFU BOFU vs. AIDA

The example in the previous section detailed the AIDA model to explain the process:

- Awareness
- Interest
- Desire
- Action

However, another explanation that you may have come across for the sale funnels is the TOFU MOFU BOFU model. I think this is an easier concept to grasp:

- TOFU – Top of the funnel
- MOFU – Middle of the funnel
- BOFU – Bottom of the funnel

Even though the idea of the funnel is that you will have more people at the top than bottom, the thought process should still be to develop a funnel that will have as many people at the bottom as possible. However, that will depend on what the goal is. Maybe you'll have fewer people but are able to generate more revenue. So, the more effective the funnel, the larger the audience in the BOFU stage or the highest revenue generated per person.

TOFU

Envision an actual funnel. When it's filled with liquid, what part of the funnel contains the most content? The top, right? The TOFU portion of the sales funnel will have the largest audience of potential leads. This would be your cold audience. Reason being is that at the very top your target audience is *everyone* you've defined. The people in this group will slowly move down and get a little narrower as you single out the interested members. This maintains as one of the largest groups of the process, as you're typically not offering anything discouraging that would make them run for the hills. In this stage, you are most likely just offering information for free without asking for anything in exchange. The good news is that online, we can capture anyone who engeges, which allows for effective progression through the funnel.

TOFU traffic or content can be both paid and organic which we will cover in more detail later, but here are some examples:

- Blogs
- Facebook
- Google+
- YouTube
- Twitter
- Pinterest
- Instagram

Remember, your goal at this stage should be to educate your audience without discouraging them with asking for exchange of anything. Some digital marketers will include opt-ins for email here, and I have done that also with some success, but since you can retarget traffic from this part of the funnel with a few of the platforms listed above and really want to have an effective nurturing process, then I recommend saving that for the next stage, MOFU.

MOFU

As the funnel narrows, you have effectively shaved off the people from the total audience that weren't interested at this particular time. This will now be your warm audience. It's important to note, however, that the members of this audience haven't been fully qualified yet. Continuing to educate is essential, as well as further positioning yourself as a solution for their specific problems or challenges. If you didn't do this at the TOFU stage, then this is the opportunity to ask for an exchange of email address for a free or a low-cost item. For health practitioners, we've had the most success with free assets in exchange for email addresses. This would be your best bet if your goal is to have them schedule an appointment. This can be private access content, white papers, videos, quiz, or download of an e-report or e-book. Anyone who opts in will allow you to add them to your inner circle community where you can nurture them to prepare them for their journey to the bottom of the funnel. Here are some examples of platforms for your MOFU nurturing:

- Email list sequences
- Private Facebook group
- Private forum on your website

BOFU

Now we're at the bottom of the funnel. This audience is hot! They have opted in. They've been nurtured and engaged through email, maybe participated and ate up everything you've provided in your private access platforms. Maybe they've even purchased a low-priced item if you went that direction. Now they have been nurtured enough, they pick up what you're putting down, they're into you and they're hungry for more. What have you got now? It's possible that at this stage you don't provide any more nurturing or content at all. For health practitioners, this is where you start trying to engage one-on-one. Propose your offer. Free phone consultation, free (which we really don't recommend) or low-cost assessment. If they take you up on your offer, you or your staff can further qualify them over the phone to make sure they are the perfect fit for your practice.

And don't forget that there is still one more part to this section as well. The prospective patient will need to successfully arrive at your practice and then start care. This takes the customer journey offline, and although we do consult with our clients here as well, we won't be covering any offline procedures in this book.

How long each person stays in each stage above depends on the individual and what the ultimate offering will be. If you are selling a $5000 health retreat, then you may have them nurture for longer in the MOFU section and have them increase their purchase capacity over time. Don't forget, however, to test all routes, as depending on your industry, some may jump right in without having to spend too much time or money nurturing.

Customer Journey vs. Sales Funnel

To recap, the purpose of the sales funnel is to attract traffic, manage and nurture the interested audience or leads, and then convert leads into paying patients or clients. The sales funnel should be thought of as a cycle, as after someone comes out the bottom, they can be retargeted for other funnels for other products and services. The customer's (aka patients or clients) journey extends beyond a single funnel. The sales funnel focuses on acquiring a customer and moving them through a process of conversion and a sale. It's a fantastic tool for selling, analytics, planning a budget, and testing the market for a particular service or product. But for the customer, the journey continues. Looking at the process from the customer's perspective and understanding that the journey includes experience and possibly multiple funnels will help to optimize your digital marketing success.

In other words, the customer journey is about understanding all pathways and experiences that potential customers follow from being a non-customer to a customer and beyond. Taking the customer journey into consideration enables you to:

- Fully understand your customer's point of view, pain points, and interests

- Think about how your customers engage with you beyond sales

- Design new services or products for other funnel processes

- Build new strategies to improve customer experience and therefore sales

- Improve your timing for the various stages of a funnel

Things have changed since the time of classical marketing. In these times of digital marketing dominance, there are many more places where a marketing campaign can touch the audience like Facebook, Twitter, YouTube, forums, blogs, etc. The emergence has expanded the customer experience, and therefore the process has become more of a journey. Not to mention the ability to re-target which returns the customer to the first step in the process of another sales funnel. The journey can be multi-channel.

The Landing Page

In a later chapter I will be covering blogs and articles, but another extremely important piece of the funnel puzzle is creating an effective landing page. This is a webpage that has the sole purpose of enticing its audience to take action. For example, opting-in for digital freebies or generating a sale of a digital product. This is something that you can build yourself on your own webpage (or have your developer do for you) or use an awesome tool like ClickFunnels. As much as I like full control of my online content and shy away from closed-source development tools like these, the biggest dog, most successful digital marketers in the world who have all the money to develop landing pages on their own website, still use these DIY page creating systems like ClickFunnels, which is the most ideal landing page creator I've seen. It's simple to use and within a couple clicks you can create multiple versions of your landing pages and run them side-by-side for testing. Having a DIY landing page creator like this is essential when trying to optimize your digital marketing initiatives.

There are many other DIY platforms, but I would argue that ClickFunnels and Leadpages are probably the two largest out there. Which is better? Well in this author's opinion, ClickFunnels checks more boxes for what we're looking for. Some bloggers are calling ClickFunnels, "Leadpages on Steroids." Which simply means the platform is jacked up! One of the challenges with marketing is figuring out what content works, for what audience, at what time. The ClickFunnels difference is that it's all about building different types of funnels through a point and click interface allowing you to test just that.

This might be sounding like an endorsement for ClickFunnels, but I can assure you that it's not. I do not get paid if you use the platform, and to further justify my argument, here are the downsides to using DIY platforms exclusively:

- The platform is not yours. And for reasons out of your control, the game can change. I'm not saying they would do that, but if we're assessing risk then I would say keeping most of your content on your own website is the way to go.
- You must ensure to use your own website domain if you're going to use these; reason being is you will be using a link to your landing page on other websites and social media. Once posted, these are permanent, so you want links with your personal or business domains floating around, not ClickFunnels or Leadpages.
- Your losing out on valuable traffic to your own website that helps with search engine optimization. You can get around this by making sure that you've set up your DIY solution properly with your own domain.

My advice in the end, is this. DO use a DIY landing page creator like ClickFunnels for sure, one that will allow you to easily create variations for testing. DON'T exclusively create content on these platforms, and make sure you keep your website because it's yours and you have the ultimate control over it.

THE NEW PATIENT GENERATOR SETUP — DAY 1 & 2

(BLOGS)

"The secret of getting ahead is getting started." – Mark Twain

Ready, Set, Go!

So, this is it! The moment you've been waiting for – first day of implementation. Just think. In only 14 days you will have built a fully functioning marketing engine that is funneling (no pun intended) countless new patients into your practice. I love to hear stories from our clients about how their life has changed once they turned the key on this machine. This has positively affected them in almost all areas of their life from family, health, their mind, financially, enjoyment at work, and socially. This can be you as well if you pay attention to the details to come and don't leave anything out.

What Is a Blog?

Honestly, I didn't even know where this term was derived from until I did a little research for this book. Apparently, blogs go all the way back to the 1990s when blogs started to appear, and the name came from the predecessor term "weblog" which was a format for websites that had news or regularly updating information that was sorted by date. As the idea gained popularity, a slang of "weblog" started to be used which turned into a Blog or Blogging, which is the act of writing and publishing a Blog. In the early 2000s blogging really started to take off with WordPress, which quickly became one of the most widely used blogging platforms on the internet.

What is the difference between a blog, a webpage, and a website you ask? That is a great question and it's important to understand. A website refers to either the full collection of webpages for a given domain like www.familyhealthadvocacy.com or www.goread. com. A webpage is a small section of the website. For example, if a website was a book then a webpage would be a chapter. And a blog is simply a webpage with a date, time, and author stamp that also incorporates the ability for the user to engage, comment, share, or interact with the website owner or blog author.

Now you're wondering how blogging is useful for marketing. The blogging platforms make it so easy to push consistent information out to your audience, and with the added benefit of interaction and sharing, it's hard to beat. In the previous chapter we talked about the concept of farming, and blogs are a fantastic way to nurture your cold and warm audiences to move them through the sales funnel. Social media, although a different category altogether, would be the only other platforms to offer this advantage for marketing, but best digital marketing practices would suggest utilizing both platforms for your customer sales journey.

Choosing Your Platform

Day 1 and 2 will be dedicated to preparing your blogs or article pages. We imagine that you're still working full time, so because this first part will require you writing about 3000 words, I think it's safe to say that we should span that across a few days.

These blogs will not try to sell your audience anything. There won't be any promotions for products or even a phone number for calling your practice for an appointment. If you remember back to the funnel organization in the previous chapter, we are at the TOFU section (Top of the Funnel). We want the biggest widest audience possible so that we can herd the interested members into the next holding area for loving, nurturing, growing, and all that good stuff. We don't want to throw anything at this audience that will make them run.

It doesn't hurt to have blogs in many places all over the internet. Your brand or yourself as an author builds credibility online the more you've spread out.

> **DID YOU KNOW?** Search engines started evaluating an author's credibility similar to how they evaluate a website's cred? Both Google and Bing confirmed that an author's authority is now being evaluated when incorporating social signals into search their results. That means that if the content that you're providing for a blog is labelling you correctly as the author and you have solid social media credibility, then your blogs will rank higher in the searches. They are calling this social authority. Their algorithms will look at how many people you follow, how many follow you, how many shares or retweets you get, number of friends, page followers you have, etc. All of this can add weight to a blog listing in the regular search results.

The benefit of this stage is that you can host these blogs or articles anywhere as long as you or your brand are credited as the author and you can have a dedicated URL or link to the page. There are many blog platforms out there but at the time of writing this book, here are the top:

WordPress
- o Considered to be the first content management or blogging system. It blew up the blogging world starting back in 2003 and is still an authority for website development and blogging today. And there are many reasons for this. In this author's opinion, WordPress is awesome! Even though on the surface it may look like a neatly organized website builder with a graphical interface so non-programmers can develop websites in minutes, but WordPress does more under the hood than that.
- o According to www.codeinwp.com WordPress powers 28 percent of the entire internet. Some other resources claim that it's 19 percent. Either way, that is huge. As of March 2016, there were 4.6 billion webpages indexed on the internet (even more if you include the dark web, but we don't want to go there. It's where the dirty illegal online black-market exists. KEEP OUT!). This means that if WordPress is responsible for 28 percent of the internet, then 1.2 billion webpages are run by the platform worldwide. These numbers are impressive, but this means that there is going to be an unbelievable amount of support with this platform which can come in handy.
- o The ability to use themes allows anyone to plug and play beautifully designed complete websites in minutes and a ton of these are free.
- o I love WordPress because of how easy you can add functionality to your webpages. You need a form for getting your audiences contact information? No problem theirs a plugin for that. You want to add a beautiful new expandable hover menu that can be both horizontal

and vertical? Gotcha covered. There's a plugin for that. Plugins for WordPress are like apps for your mobile phone. They allow you to enhance your webpages with almost limitless functionality.

o   Another cool feature included with WordPress is it comes out the box with the ability to have a user community! It's super easy to set up a members-only website with plugins. Some are free, and some charge a minimal fee so you can just choose which ones suit your needs the best. With this functionality, you can use your website to create private content that you can use to build your email list or even make money.

o   The best part... WordPress is FREE! Obviously, that gets you just the basics, but you can get started for free and then even when you've outgrown the freebie functionality, the cost is very minimal to expand. Did I mention that I love this platform?

o   What about blogging? This is the whole point of WordPress in the first place. No matter which theme you choose for your website, whether its hosted for free at WordPress.com, hosted for a minimal charge at WordPress.org, or you have your own hosting using the WordPress platform, all comes with the plug-in-play ability to easily publish or update blog articles. And they are formatted correctly so they stay friendly with the search engines.

o   Pitfalls of WordPress worth mentioning: Security. Nothing is perfect, and WordPress doesn't escape that fact. I will preface this by saying that WordPress itself is very secure if the WordPress security best practices are followed. Does the average WordPress site follow the best practices? Probably not. This leaves those websites vulnerable to hackers. And if I'll be honest, our WordPress websites have been hacked a few times. Although it was frustrating to resolve, we locked it all down and secured the back doors while learning a valuable lesson. I almost take it as a compliment because we had enough daily traffic to our website that we were targeted by a traffic hacker. We made it! I won't list all the precautions here as I'd like to move on, but you can easily find all the tips you need to make sure your WordPress website is secured like Fort Knox.

o If my opinion isn't obvious to you at this point, WordPress would be my number one pick for your main blogging platform and website.

Wix

o Although considered to be more of a website development tool due to its Freemium revenue structure (Free to use but charges for premium upgrades) and it's simple to use drag and drop website builder, Wix websites have a blogging framework built right in just like WordPress. You don't have to know any coding to develop a beautiful, fully responsive website (responsive means that the website will re-format depending on which device a user is viewing your website from. Either a computer with a large monitor, smaller screen on a tablet, or on a mobile phone).

o What's cool about Wix is that you can get started with a website template that is geared for your industry. If you're a healthcare practitioner, you can find a great starting point template that is styled and functional for your needs.

o They now can even one-up the use of the template! They also offer something called Artificial Design Intelligence (ADI) – imagine being asked a few questions about your business and with the click of a button your whole website is designed and laid out. This is what Wix brings to you with their ADI system. Get started right away and don't worry about paying some developer $10,000+ for a fully custom website until you really need it.

o Wix comes complete with a blogger's toolkit. Write new posts, edit drafts, schedule upcoming posts, spread your content with simple social media tools, apply tags and categorize, easily include media like videos and photos, allow further engagement with member or guest comments, and even customize with the ability to embed your own code for the slightly advanced user.

o Pitfalls of Wix: At the time of writing this book, Wix still included advertisements on their starting plan websites. If you want your site free and clear of ads then you would need to upgrade. As simple as it is to use, perfecting your site will take time. As much as the marketing material promotes the contrary, some users might have been over-promised and under-delivered in that department. The biggest complaint I have is the limitation of apps and plug-ins. For the average blogger this might not be important, but when you really want to customize or add functionality down the road, you will be limited without having to rebuild your website outside the Wix platform. Same goes if you ever want to move your website from Wix, it would have to be rebuilt.

Blogger

o According to Wikipedia, "Blogger is a blog-publishing service that allows multi-user blogs with time-stamped entries. It was developed by Pyra Labs, which was bought by Google in 2003. Generally, the blogs are hosted by Google at a subdomain of blogspot.com. Blogs can also be hosted in the registered custom domain of the blogger (like www.johndoe.com). A user can have up to 100 blogs per account."

o Did you read that? Blogger is Google's blog-publishing service. Considering Google is the search engine of choice for the entire world and Google likes to reward the use of its own services, then if you're considering to get started with Blogging then Blogger could be a great FREE option. It's easy to use and might be the simplest of the top 3 on this list. There is no setup required, hosting is free, and you get a custom domain with the BlogSpot.com subdomain. Another great feature is your blog pages will be secured by Google. If they get really popular, then you can be assured they will be safe. You can also earn money from your blog with Google AdSense integration.

- o Pitfalls of Blogger: With the Blogger platform, you have limited options to modify and customize. Even though they provide templates, they are limited. Also, at the time of writing this book, they capped the number of blogs you can have per account to 100. Moving the blogs off the platform will pose problems with any search "juice" you've developed and copying the content to another site and having duplicates will hurt the blogs' search credibility as well. With this option you don't have complete control over your blog, and Google can pull the rug from underneath you at any time. These are all things to consider. However, as I mentioned earlier, it helps your author credibility to have popular content all over the internet, so producing blog content on this platform in addition to your own personal websites and linking them would be an effective strategy long term.

Tumblr
- o Have you heard of it? Maybe and maybe not. Well it's considered to be the hottest blogging platform for the younger generation, and considering Tumblr's growth over the years, it has the potential to explode your content with viral blogging.
- o Tumblr combines the best of two worlds: blogging and social media. You have the ability to strictly use it for either, but the magic for Tumblr is when you combine

both. It's platform is quite simple to use and you have the ability to build a community around your content. With user experience at the forefront, successful blogs here tend to be shorter and more visual with media-like photos, animations, and videos.

o   One valuable tool that Tumblr can be used for is to identify trends. Choosing the right topic at the right time is important for blog success, so understanding the current trends in order to tie them into your topic is something that you can use Tumblr to help you with. What's cool is that a Tumblr post can go viral within hours, spreading all over the internet. What do you think that would do for your author credibility?

o   Pitfalls for Tumblr: Some claim that the platform's downfall is that users can repost other people's content by copy/pasting or downloading and then creating brand new posts on other platforms as their own original material. Well this is true for all social media, and the whole internet for that matter. Just know that copyright laws apply for most countries, and if you discover that your work has been stolen, then you would be protected legally. However, enforcing this can be a real pain. I consider this to be a weak criticism as it's not unique to the platform but something to consider nonetheless.

o   The other pitfall is the ability for users to comment anonymously. It's too easy for users to abuse this feature and become cyber-bullies. Luckily you have the option to turn this feature off and not allow anonymous commenting.

Ghost, Medium

o   There are other great tools to use for blogging as well; however, I won't go into as much detail with these. Both Ghost and Medium are popular alternatives to the abovementioned platforms. As you can probably begin to understand, each have pros and cons of their own. It's all about simplicity, and if a platform can produce a high-quality blog page that is easy to use, it's going to be a winner.

o   Ghost is a simple platform that boasts a crisp minimal user interface. It's more comparable to Google's Blogger than a full-blown platform like WordPress or Wix. Its biggest downfall, similar to Blogger, is that it's limited in what you can do beyond simple blog articles.

o   Medium is a blogging platform community in which they define themselves as "a community of readers and writers offering unique perspectives on ideas large and small." The platform caters to longform writing on niche topics. For healthcare practitioners for example, it's great for writing about a specific condition or research around a health topic as it's considered to be niche-centric blogging for no cost.

Squarespace, Weebly

o   These are the other popular do-it-yourself website builders that can be used for blogging. They both offer a "drag and drop" interface for simple content presentation just like Wix. However, like Wix, if you ever decide to switch platforms, it's not easy and in most cases you'll have to start from scratch. The other problem which we outlined above is that these services are considered "closed-source," meaning the public can't contribute to expanding their functionality like WordPress. This means that you're limited in functionality options. That doesn't mean that they won't try to grow and add on to their functionality, but they are certainly developed and presented at a slower rate than a platform that has the world at their disposal for new features. As a techy nerd, that makes me want to scream. I want an easy to use system with maximum functionality coupled with ultimate control. You do not get that with the DIY platforms like these.

Who Likes Traffic?

I do! Traffic in my car on the highway; not so much. Traffic on my blogs, however; can't wipe the smile off my face. So far, I've explained what a blog is, why it's useful for marketing, and the different platforms you can use. Coming up in the implementation step-by-step section we'll talk further about content creation. However, having a website packed with amazing blogs without any traffic is like having a giant Walmart in a one-horse ghost town. Useless. It is extremely important to prepare consistent and relevant blog content, but really you need traffic for the blog to work its magic. Traffic can either be bought or generated organically through search engines. I would say that most people would prefer organic traffic because it appears cheaper. Makes sense but it's also harder to come by. Search Engine Optimization (SEO) is such a hot topic for this reason. Optimizing your webpages and blog articles so that they rank high for specific keywords in search engines like Google, is not easy and takes time. It's almost a grand mystery like understanding how God works in relation to our world (if that's your belief) when trying to decode how a major search engine like Google ranks their webpages. The biggest challenge, as it is very complex, is not about doing one thing right. It's about doing hundreds of things right with some things out of your control. If you come up with the most amazing business and want to flood traffic to your blogs and website right away, the fastest route to get there isn't going to be Search Engine Optimization (SEO). Because it's so complicated, you'll most likely have to hire an expert in the field, who do not come cheap. You'll spend a ton of money to put everything in place and your return on investment may come years down the road, if ever. The good news about most blogging platforms is that they've got you covered for the most part. Save your money for more important things, and know that by simply being consistent with exciting content and a few simple SEO tips and tricks, you will do just fine. I *do* suggest that you invest in paid traffic, however, if you want to get the ball rolling quick. We will cover that later in this book.

Step 1: Topic Research

This is a very important step, and if you skip it, you may end up wasting your time and money. What you think may be the hottest topic for your industry just might not be the reality. For example, I work with many chiropractors, and what is the first thing that comes to mind when brainstorming the best topic to focus on? If you know anything about the profession, then you're probably thinking back pain. The trick with finding the best topics to focus on is to potentially ignore what first comes to mind. With a little research you'll find that back pain (as prevalent as it is) is not even in the top three of conditions that the general public are seeking answers for. A simple investigation using Google's Keyword Planner Tool will give you insights that show a specific keyword as well as related ones and how often they are searched within an indicated time period. Start here!

Go to Google Keyword Planner and discover what the top 6 searched topics around your profession are and list them here:

1. _____

2. _____

3. _____

4. _____

5. _____

6. _____

Now to further refine your topics you can discover how to link them to current trends in the market. For example, let's say that a famous athlete, "Joey Baseball" just got busted for using a performance-enhancing drug such as an anabolic steroid and has been getting a lot of publicity, also meaning that it's being searched rigorously. To help with the searchability of one of your blog's top 6 topics listed above, you will want to tie it into this current trend. To explain further, let's say that one of your top topics is "building lean muscle." Combining all this information together helps you create a powerhouse of a blog article. Something like "The Truth about Anabolic Steroids and Building Lean Muscle" might be the way to go.

Google also has a great research tool for this called Google Trends, but there are many more that you may find useful to help with this part of your research.

Go to Google Trends and discover what the top 6 current trends are around your profession and topics listed above and list them here:

1. _____

2. _____

3. _____

4. _____

5. _____

6. _____

Step 2: Choose Your Blog Platform.

Now that you're armed with information, it's time to set up your blog platform. Choose from the list of platforms mentioned in the previous section. Each of them have their own tutorials on how to use them and how to set them up so I won't be going into detail about those here. It's possible that many of you have your own website already, and if so, then I hope that it was developed on a blogging platform. If that is the case, then you can just skip ahead to the next section.

If you have a website that was not built on a blogging framework, then I recommend that you upgrade immediately. Even worse is that it's most likely programmed archaically and might not even be responsive for all devices. This is a search engine ranking destroyer. Upgrade immediately! But while you're waiting to set up your new website, I would get started writing your blog content today and just host it on Blogger. We don't want to delay this powerful new patient machine asset any longer.

Step 3: Choose 6 of the most popular, aggravating, pressing topics or pain points that your ideal patient or client is faced with – the ones that you have the solution for.

Most likely you will use the top 6 searched topics within your profession you discovered in step 1 of this chapter, but maybe not. Maybe you would like to specialize in a specific area like Paediatric or Geriatric branches of the topic. The idea is that we're going to continue to create blogs around these topics down the road, but to get started let's get one done for each of them. You can write them here:

1. _____

2. _____

3. _____

4. _____

5. _____

6. _____

Examples:

1. Numbness or tingling in the hands or feet
2. Teeth Whitening
3. Headaches or Migraines
4. Attention Deficit Disorder
5. Depression
6. Obesity

Step 4: Write Catchy Titles Your Audience Can't Resist.

Time to get creative! However, use this list to help get started:

How to …   The Great _____ Hoax

Quick Guide to…   [Number] Creative Ways to…

Complete…   BREAKING NEWS! …

Ultimate...

Beginners...

Hacked...

DIY...

The Anatomy of...

[Number] Things You
Thought You Knew...

What You Should NOT do...

[Number] No nonsense...

Top [number] Ways to...

Secret Solutions for...

Everything You've Been
Taught About _____ is wrong!

1. _____

2. _____

3. _____

4. _____

5. _____

6. _____

7. _____

8. _____

9. _____

10. _____

Examples:

1. How to Heal Numbness or Tingling without Drugs or Surgery
2. The Ultimate DIY Teeth Whitening Solution
3. What You Should NOT Do if You Experience Headaches or Migraines
4. Everything You've Been Taught About Attention Deficit Disorder is Wrong
5. The Anatomy of Depression
6. The TOP 6 Secret Solutions for Losing 20 lbs in 30 Days

Step 5: The Anatomy of the Perfect Health Blog. (It's time to get writing!)

It's time to get writing. If you are going to produce 10 articles in 5 days, then you're probably wondering how long each article must be. Even though the ideal blog length depends on its purpose, for us, health practitioners, we want to steer more towards a longer article than a short one without boring the heck out of your audience. This is the time to showcase the depth of your knowledge, so it's more about hitting all the necessary points than worrying about the length. However, if you have effectively nailed the outline I'm about to give you, then you will have probably written 500 words or more. Simple math tells us that you will be writing 5000 words over the 5 days. Think you can do it? Of course you can! Let's get to it. I've included the following article builder that I developed to help you get started. Building future articles for each topic, you'll probably have to change up the format, but as long as you keep the content current, relevant, and highlighting yourself as the expert, then it will do the trick. Also, it's important to give lots of value for FREE. For now, simply answer these questions in as much detail as you can, piece the answers together, and voila, you've got yourself a rockin' health blog that is optimized for nurturing your cold and warm audiences. Repeat for each additional blog until you have 10 complete.

1. List ALL the extenuating complications that can result by the condition or problem

    a. _____

    b. _____

    c. _____

    d. _____

    e. _____

    f. _____

    g. _____

2. How many other people in your city, province/state, or the world suffer from this condition or problem?
3. In your professional opinion, what are the causes of this condition or problem?
4. What are things that people try to do to remedy this condition or problem that have not been effective? Think about treatments for the extenuating complications of the condition as well.
5. What information do you have that is different than the other ineffective approaches listed above?
6. What are some DIY tips your audience can do to start helping themselves (most likely they won't do them and somewhere down the funnel they'll be opting in for an examination in your practice)?
7. Please list some articles or research references that show how your approach is effective for the condition or problem.
8. Obtain one or two testimonials from current patients that you can embed in the blog article.

Example Blog Article Written for a Chiropractor:

Title:

If your life is afflicted by numbness or tingling in the arms, hands, fingers, legs, feet, or toes then you will be interested in this clinical study that showed...

How Patients Significantly Improved Their Sharp Pains, Grip Strength, and Eliminated Numbness and Tingling Without Drugs or Surgery

Body:

Numbness, tingling, and pain affects all parts of your life

Numbness and tingling is a huge problem, which affects every part of your life from sleeping, sitting, or walking. The thought of getting a good night's sleep or playing with your kids or grandchildren may seem like a pipe dream because your arms or legs are in too much pain and may even be weak.

Maybe you're frustrated because you've been told that you must live with it, as all the medical testing indicates that you shouldn't have a problem. Or maybe you're even fearful because the only options left are drugs with heavy side effects or surgery.

I can tell you one thing...you are not alone. Millions of people suffer from some form of peripheral neuropathy, which can be caused by different things. It is described by webmd.com as a condition that results when nerves from the brain and spinal cord, which carry messages to and from the rest of the body are damaged or diseased.

This condition obstructs the nerve signals that control your muscles, joints, connective tissues, and organs, and if ignored, could lead to more serious complications.

"I feel like I'm 30 years older than I actually am. I can't walk great distances without pain. My hands go numb while doing the simplest activities like watching TV or lying in bed. I am tired of living this way."

Here are my top 9 natural solutions to numbness and tingling in which I will go into further detail on another blog so keep an eye out for it, but if you have any questions, please feel free to add your comments below:

1. Chiropractic
2. Warm Compress or Heating Pad
3. Self Massage
4. Physical Activity
5. Tumeric
6. Epsom Salt
7. Cinnamon
8. Vitamin B
9. Magnesium

More Pills Are Not the Solution

My name is [name] from [practice] in [city]. I have been helping people with nerve related conditions for over [number] years. I want to let you know that there is hope, and you do have another option in Chiropractic that has been proven effective in removing pressure on the nerves without drugs or surgery.

There have been many clinical studies which have demonstrated the benefit of chiropractic and nerve conditions:

Patients showed an 85.5 percent resolution of the nerve symptoms after only 9 chiropractic treatments. – Journal of Chiropractic Medicine 2008

With chiropractic care, patients had "significant improvement in perceived comfort and function, nerve conduction, and finger sensation overall." – JMPT 1998

"Significant increase in grip strength and normalization of motor and sensory latencies were noted. Orthopedic tests were negative. Symptoms dissipated." – JMPT 1994

What these studies mean is that there is hope for you to get your life back.

Where should you start?

Finding the cause of your neuropathy is where you should start. The doctor of chiropractic is trained to identify the causes of neuropathic conditions, and if your case is beyond the scope of chiropractic, you would be referred to the appropriate health professional. However, often these conditions are caused by a degeneration or misalignment of the spine, which can press on the roots of the nerves. This pressure can arise from the bones or intervertebral discs anywhere on the spine from the base of the head down to the tail bone.

Whether you have been to a chiropractor before or this would be your first experience, you may be wondering what to expect with us. We want you to understand everything about your case and our procedures before we get started. Our exams are thorough and our patients describe our techniques as "gentle and effective." We have many techniques that we can use to ensure that you are comfortable without hindering the results of your care and progress.

The goal is to release pressure on the nerves to allow your body to heal.

Example 2 Blog Article Written for a Chiropractor:

Title:

Top 5 Reasons Why You Can't Get Rid of Your Headaches

Body:

Have you ever experienced, or are you currently suffering from dreaded headaches or migraines?

There can be many causes of headaches and even more reasons why you aren't getting relief from your pain.

What have you done to relieve your pain?

Many people try to use hot or cold compresses to relieve their headaches, use pain killers, and even have to go to bed for the rest of the day because of their pain. While these therapies are common to relieve symptoms once they have started, it is important to find ways to prevent headaches and migraines and understand why you may be unable to heal your pain.

Here, we will identify the Top 5 Reasons Why You May be Unable to Heal Your Pain:

1. Vitamins and Minerals Deficiency

If your body is deficient in essential vitamins, minerals, fatty acids, or antioxidants, it will be very difficult to effectively heal. Your body needs to be provided with abundant nutrients from various sources to fulfill your daily fuel requirements.

Your diet should consist of a variety of colors, with a base color of many greens and adding in reds, oranges, yellows, blues, and purples. If you focus on eating 80 percent fruits or vegetables at every meal, you will be on your way to fulfilling your color and nutrient requirements.

Include fresh green salads into your day with lettuce, spinach, kale, and add red/yellow/orange peppers, carrots, grapes, cucumbers, and all your favourite vegetables for color and nutrient value.

2. Insufficient, Poor-Quality Sleep

How many hours of quality, uninterrupted sleep do you squeeze in per night? If you're getting less than eight, then this could be impacting your health and heightening your sensitivity to pain.

Your body needs to experience deep, uninterrupted, quality sleep to reap the restorative benefits of this resting time.

If you have trouble falling asleep, try turning off your electronics and dimming your lights at least one hour before your bedtime goal. The light from your devices skews your circadian rhythm and prevents you from realizing that it is bedtime.

Sleep Goal: Go to sleep not long after sunset and rise with the sun!

3. Lack of Movement

Our bodies were designed to move. But our sedentary lifestyles have taken over, and too many hours at the computer, at our desks, and in front of the television have changed our ancestral ways of hunting and gathering to stumbling to the fridge and then back to your chair.

It's incredibly important to build regular exercise into your schedule. Speak to your natural health practitioner about what would be the best ways to get started, but really, whatever you can manage while you are in pain to move your body is great. Start off slowly and build up to your goals. Go for short walks, do some yoga stretches, or any exercise that feels good to you.

4. Pharmaceutical Overload

A common treatment for pain is a prescription for pharmaceuticals. They do work for short term relief however, overuse can often negatively impact your overall health. Inflammation is often a cause of chronic pain, and we must work to eliminate inflammation rather than contribute to it. It is important to find long term natural solutions that work to boost up your body rather than abusing treatments designed for short term relief which could have an extensive list of potential side effects.

5. Nervous System Interference

Your nerve system controls every single aspect of your body, from breathing to digestion to cell division. Your brain sends messages to every single part of your body and they travel via your central nerve system, which is encased by the bones of your spine.

If any of your spinal bones shift out of alignment, it puts pressure on your nerve system, and your brain is unable to efficiently send all the messages it needs to, to every cell, organ, and tissue of your body. The messages that your brain sends out to direct healing can be halted or interfered with, and this can cause headaches to continue or intensify because the healing messages are not able to reach their destination.

The best way to detect these misalignments of your spine is to have an examination with a chiropractor, who can determine a program of care to correct your spine and help to reduce or eliminate your pain.

It is essential to discover the root cause of your headache and migraine symptoms and allow your body to heal naturally. Don't ignore your symptoms and do nothing.

Step 6: Publish Your Blogs.

Fantastic! You've got your 10 blog articles created, but they're not going to work that well sitting on your computer. You've got to publish them. By now you should have chosen your platforms, whether it's on your own website or one of the free options I mentioned previously. After you've published your content online, then make a note of their URL or webpage address and add them here. You will need these later when we're setting up your paid traffic sources:

1. _____

2. _____

3. _____

4. _____

5. _____

6. _____

7. _____

8. _____

9. _____

10. _____

THE NEW PATIENT GENERATOR SETUP – DAY 3, 4 & 5

(SOCIAL MEDIA)

"Shoot for the moon, if you miss then you'll land in the stars."
– Unknown

Brace Yourself

Brace yourself. The rollercoaster is going over the top. This section is huge. Social Media is a massive topic and whole books have been written on this alone. It's difficult to determine the exact number of social network websites or platforms worldwide, but according to smartinsights.com, the top 22 boast a user base of 10 billion active users in January 2017. No wonder why marketing has become a major source of revenue when you think of the number of eyes using these platforms per day. When compared to television, the total numbers of eyes and ears worldwide is greater still, but there are many disadvantages from a marketing perspective with TV, Radio, and Print when compared to online. The first is the expense. I realize that if you have some interesting news then it's possible to present a press release for free. However, it's not guaranteed to be covered. You could appear on talk shows as a guest; however, even if you land a spot, most likely the broadcast will be so infrequent that it doesn't really help you for a long-term initiative. This makes it virtually impossible to build a following or a community for your practice with these forms of media unless you're paying big bucks. Even if you're willing to pay, these avenues are limited. The audience reach is very broad, the audience share is generally declining, the ability to digitally record has impacted the effect of commercials, typically the costs are high, and most lack the ability for engagement.

The social media platforms online are quite the contrary. You can win with both sides of the coin. If you're willing to pay, then you can reach a lot people that can be highly targeted to produce an audience of almost perfect customers or patients. Beyond that, you can build free engagement platforms for your practice that will allow you to interact with your community. Although we will be detailing both dimensions of social media in this book, for this chapter, we will be talking about:

- the most important platforms for your practice
- how to nurture existing patients to grow them into super-patients who refer
- how to build your external health community
- how to keep the external community engaged and ascend them to start care in your practice

Note in chapters to follow we will cover sponsored advertising, aka paid advertising, for your practice.

The Top 6 Social Media Platforms You Need for Your Practice

Six? Let me guess you're already finding it challenging to manage content for one and there are six I'm suggesting? How on earth are you going to do that? It all comes down to planning, automation, and using all the resources you have available. Within a month, the new patient generator you're currently building will be starting to increase your revenue so much that you can afford to hire someone to manage it for you. If you can take the time within these two weeks to get a couple months automated, and you or your staff dedicate 5-10 minutes per day to keep the conversation going, then these farming style marketing initiatives will help you explode your practice that much sooner.

I will provide more detail about the implementation in the following sections, but for now let's take the time to go through each platform in detail, so you understand why each are important to include in your new patient generator machine. They each have their own benefit and vary in user base demographics.

Facebook

- o The juggernaut of social media. Unless you've been living with a lost Myan tribe deep in the Guatemalan jungle for the last 15 years, you've probably heard of it. Brought to the forefront of the internet in 2004, Facebook has grown to be the largest social media platform online with an astonishing 2 billion users in June of 2017 according to zephoria.com. This sets up the perfect environment for marketing of any business. However, like TV and Radio, what brings people to the platform isn't the advertising. It's all the other goodies they have to offer their audience. Although the largest demographic on Facebook is aged 25 to 34, this platform has one of the most diverse demographics for its users when compared to the others. This makes Facebook a perfect marketing nesting ground for health practices specializing in helping people of all ages.

- o Why is Facebook so Popular?

  - ▪ *It's so easy to set up and use* – Although still more popular with under 40s, Facebook's simple interface allows for users of all ages to take part in the fun. It's jam packed with amazing social features that somehow are presented very light-weight.

- *Tons of Entertaining Features* – With an ample amount of games, applications, videos, and images, people are turning to this platform for their regular entertainment. When I grew up, and wasn't kicked outside to enjoy the beautiful day by my parents, it was TV or console video games that kept my attention. Not today. So many people of all ages are turning to Facebook for their daily dose of fun and entertainment.

- *Connecting with old Friends* – I'll have to admit, back in mid 2000s as Facebook was growing, I tried to avoid the "fad" and stayed as far away from Facebook as possible. But what got me hooked was that I had a whole bunch of old friends whom I hadn't connected with in a very long time add me on the platform. I was so intrigued and couldn't resist. Now I'm a long-time user of the platform, not to mention revolving my whole career around it. I do believe that you increase your chances of success the more connections you have in life, and I don't know any easier to way to connect than Facebook.

- *The News Feed* – Primarily a way to maintain connections and engage socially, Facebook has become a major source of information or news that is current and relevant to you. But not just news from the news agencies, anything and everything that any of your Facebook Friends wants the world to know. The feed loads like a vertical bulletin board that is enhanced with images, videos, audio, and questionnaires, so naturally this is where the majority of the 2 billion

THE NEW PATIENT GENERATOR

users are planting their eyes. Now imagine you could slip in a relevant post of information in there about your service or practice? That's the power of using Facebook for internal and external marketing. Even better, you get to have a say! The days of yelling at your TV when you watch something that gets the blood boiling are over. With Facebook, you can pipe in and let your opinion be heard.

o Facebook Foundations for Your Practice

- Profiles – The Facebook Profile represents a single individual and they ensure that you won't be using it for commercial use. If you get caught using a profile for business, then Facebook will shut it down. It's against Facebook's Terms of Policy to create a personal account for a business. You will have to use one of the other foundations mentioned here as an entity for your practice. Don't have a personal Facebook Profile yet? Get one. They're free and easy to set up. You can use it to connect with old friends, yes, but more importantly you can connect with your current patients, prospective patients from your community, and other health professionals as well for networking. Also, Facebook requires all Business Pages (detailed next) to be linked to a personal account so that they can administrate the Page. Actually, to set up the next two foundations listed here, you or maybe your staff must have a personal profile. From your profile, you will have the ability to upload photos and let the world know about you on a personal level. This is important for humanizing yourself, as the public is considering joining any online communities that you run. You are also able to accept and send private messages as yourself rather than your business, which will also be helpful for communication down the road. Most importantly, you can expand your online presence by using that profile to engage online. Comment, react to posted information, and share content that you feel would be helpful for your friends and online community. Bottom line. You, as a health practitioner, need a Facebook Personal Profile if you don't have one.

- Pages – Another necessity for your practice. These are like a personal profile; however, it allows the ability to have an organization such as a charity or business, brand, or public figure to have similar functionality within Facebook as Profiles do. However, you can also share promotions, offer specials, and make announcements with the goal of building a fan base for your practice. Another added benefit is that anyone who "likes" or follows your page will have information you post show up in their feed. This gives the ability for your practice to expand it's community beyond the connections you've made within your personal profile. The term "Organic Reach" is used when referring to the number of people that a page post will be presented to in their newsfeed. You would think that 100 percent of your followers should see the information your page is posting, but unfortunately, Facebook continues to kibosh the ability to do this without charging you. There are some tips and tricks to help increase your organic reach, like using Facebook Live to deliver messages; however, down the road I think Facebook will favor paid reach for everything. The good news is that Facebook makes it much more affordable to get your information out there when compared to the conventional platforms like TV, radio, and print, which means you should be able to easily see a very positive ROI rendering this as not a major problem. In the end, the biggest benefits of having a page for your practice is to have another way for communicating privately with patients and your community, the ability to post, comment and share all as your practice entity. It's another place to find out information about your practice like hours of operation, location, and upcoming events. Engaging as your page increases your practice's online exposure, but also the more information you present and the more people that follow you, the more social credibility your practice will have. This is important when people who are on the fence about joining your community are doing their research about you. The more cred you have, the greater the chance they're going to jump on board.

- Groups – In our experience of working with health practitioners across many professions, this is the feature that is not used to its full potential. Possibly because most don't understand the difference with a group and the advantages that a group offers. A group is almost like hanging out with people in a confer-ence room and they can be either public or private. Both types of groups are a benefit to you as a health practitioner and I will explain the differences. For any business, Facebook Groups are a powerful tool. Going back to the analogy of a conference room, imagine a massive room with hundreds of people each with a microphone, but YOU'RE at the front standing at the podium. If you're a dentist who specializes in children for example, then imagine the room filled with mothers or fathers eager to learn more about paediatric dentistry. You now have a place to position yourself as the expert in your community for a given topic. You can find an existing public group and join the conversation, or create a free public group and work to fill it with interested people in your community. You can even monetize a private support group if you want. The benefits of these groups are that the people in them are generally looking for answers and are highly targeted. It's worth noting that if you don't own the group then you will have to adhere to the group owner's rules and restrictions and many groups do not let you solicit business. I would say that as general rule of thumb it's best just to pop into various groups that you don't own where you can offer information for free. This farming technique will contribute to your authority on a subject and will plant seeds. The more seeds you plant, the larger the crop you will harvest. Want to play by your own rules? Then you will have to create your own group. You can make a private group for many reasons, including promotion of products or a condition/topic focused group. The latter would be the preferred route for farming potential new patients or clients.

Instagram

o   This platform, also owned by Facebook (the king of social media), is considered to be the queen. Although maintaining much of the same social functionality as its partner in social royalty, Instagram is all about media. Posting, categorizing (aka hash tagging), sharing, and commenting that all revolves around images and videos with easy ways to spruce them up and make them fun with filters. The platform caters to an audience of people who love the visual, and now with the introduction of Instagram Stories, you can take your followers on a journey through all the moments of your day through video and images, which is what makes this such an awesome tool for both internal and external digital marketing of your practice. Understanding the demographics of each social media platform is important. That will determine how much content you produce for each. All the same advantages apply here though, like the social credibility that comes with a decent following, so having an Instagram account that is regularly updated is a must and should not be ignored. The good news is that you can create a business account on Instagram if you already have a Facebook Page for your business. Either you, or most likely your staff, should be using their mobile devices throughout each day or pick a day of the week to take videos and pictures showing the day in progression. You shouldn't really keep it all business. Mixing in simple fun things with patient stories or testimonials is really the winning strategy. You can also tag people to help extend your reach.

o   To further explain the benefit, let's walk through a practical scenario of how this farming technique can even generate new patients for your practice if not educate them. Let's say you're a registered acupuncturist and you have a client named Mary. Mary is a great patient. She is on Facebook and Instagram regularly and follows your practice on both. On Fridays, you've decided that you're going to create a story of your day in practice. One of the items included for the story was a video testimonial of a patient named Sam who has had an amazing thing happen. She finally got pregnant after starting care with you! Mary, another patient who saw the video, was blown away as she didn't even know that your acupuncture could help with that, and she immediately thinks of her sister who lives in the area and has almost given up on having a child, thinking she's maybe infertile. What does Mary do? She shares the video with her sister who is thrilled, and because she has access to all your contact information right there on your business profile, she contacts you for an appointment. Remember, farming is all about planting seeds and with this part of the new patient generator machine that you will have created at the end of this book, you'll have set up a 200 acre farm!

o   The other bonus is hashtagging, which simply refers to a way to categorize your posts. Similar to twitter and hashtagging tweets, which we will go over shortly, you can add your posts to a specific trending hashtag category or create a brand new one. There is so much power with this as a health practitioner, as many users like to view the feeds around a specific topic. If you're a dentist and you posted a cool video on teeth whitening with the hashtag, #teethwhitening and are the most recent person or organization to use that hashtag, then your post will be at the top of the list if someone is searching that out. Pretty cool!

o   One bummer with Instagram is that it doesn't stretch across age groups like Facebook yet. At the time of writing this book, the contingent of users is mainly between 18-29 years old. However, it's growing and growing fast and that doesn't mean that the platform is void of the other age groups either. They are there too, just in lower numbers, and they still need seeds planted for them.

YouTube

o   YouTube, as you know, is the Godfather for video online. They boast over 1.3 billion users and have over 30 million users viewing videos on their site each and every day. This is massive! Surveys are now saying that 6 out of 10 people would prefer to watch their videos online versus traditional TV, so the takeover is well underway. YouTube is not viewed as a traditional social media platform, as you do not need an account to enjoy the close to 1 billion hours of video available for viewing. This, combined with the fact that Google owns this mega platform and heavily includes videos into the top search ranking positions on given topics, makes this an essential tool for your farming and hunting marketing initiatives.

o   I'm sure you've heard the concept of a viral video. It's a video posted that zooms to hundreds of millions of views, sometimes within days. According to Statista.com, the fastest viral video so far is Facebook's Ring – Hidden Camera Prank, which hit 200 million views in a mere 24 hours. Pretty impressive. However, as cool as a viral video for your practice would be, that's not really the goal we're going to outline here. We are going to have you create a YouTube channel for your practice, record quality, compelling, relevant videos around the most pressing topics for your profession, make sure that your video can be found by people in your community, and then build subscribers.

o   Think of it this way. Future patients or clients of yours are already on YouTube with most of them there every single day. It's probably a good idea to get your face on there.

Twitter

o   This platform was one of the first since Facebook to revolutionize the social experience. Its simple 140 max character "tweets" are presented for the whole world to see as opposed to requiring a connection between users.

Information across an endless sea of categories is made searchable through the adoption of the hashtag which really exploded the Twitter concept.

Interesting Note: The hashtag idea wasn't invented by Twitter. Some dude over at Google first spouted the idea to them back in 2007. He suggested they use the idea to categorize their Tweet content. Funny enough Twitter originally rejected the idea, and he was quoted by the Wall Street Journal as saying "[Twitter] told me flat out, these things are for nerds. They're never going to catch on."

o Currently Twitter has over 328 million users that tweet over 500 million times per day. Unlike Instagram, the spread in age demographic covers more ground, making it a competitive player for health practitioners specializing in all ages.

o However, you may have heard that Twitter tends to get flack for its paid advertising revenues which is failing to keep Wall Street happy. There has even been speculation about what the future holds for this massive social platform. I doubt it's going anywhere, as I'm sure they'll figure it out. If they can keep growing their user base, then they can justify going the direction of Facebook and slowly becoming a pay-to-play platform for exposure. I've read it's already happening and the organic reach for your tweets is not what it once was. With all that being said, I don't suggest you ignore the platform. There is still a lot that you can do for free and a large following lends to your online credibility or social proof. Also, anyone who is actively searching hashtag topics can come across your past tweets and take action, and lets not forget Twitter

Chats, a powerful tool for health practitioners to share their voice around a topic of their expertise.

o Twitter Chat is considered to be the secret weapon for getting your voice heard on Twitter. It's an online event where moderators open discussions around a specific topic using the hashtag system. These sessions often follow a question and answer format allowing participants to voice their opinions, offer solutions, or present feedback.

o You can see how this would be beneficial as a health practitioner. You can choose chats that are relevant to your profession, and by providing useful answers on a regular basis, this increases your exposure by the right people who in the future could connect with you for help. This is another useful seed-planting tool for your surrounding community.

Pinterest, LinkedIn

o These platforms, although quite popular, you may choose to omit. I'm not discrediting these sites at all and they are powerful tools. However, we won't be going into very much detail on them.

o For the purposes of farming new patients for a health practice, I believe that Pinterest is probably the better of the two, and if you have a personal interest in making creative health memes, like giving exercise tips or posting recipes, then Pinterest would be one to add to your farming marketing initiatives.

o LinkedIn I would say is the least appropriate social media platform for farming prospective patients. It is an amazing platform for networking and connecting with other health practitioners but the objective with the users is much different here than the day-to-day activities of the other top social platforms. However, LinkedIn might come in handy for your practice for hiring staff.

On Day 3, 4, and 5, we'll be spending the time setting up all your organic social media platforms and content. Remember that building this portion is all part of the farming techniques that was discussed in earlier chapters. The main objectives here are to nurture your existing patient or fan base, increase your online presence or exposure, boost your social credibility, and give your author authority some clout to help improve your blog's search rankings. Please note that each social platform has even further detail within its own documentation in case you feel like we didn't go deep enough. Here we go!

Step 1: Ensure you have created the correct accounts for all the social platforms we've discussed in this chapter.

Whether you're gearing up to start your business on social media or just need to add one or two accounts, the following is a checklist of what you will need to have set up. Make sure that you set them up in the order shown:

(1) Facebook Personal Profile

(2) Facebook Page

(3) Instagram Business Page

- Make sure you're logged into Facebook when you begin this process so that you can easily link your information. You won't need a potentially redundant personal Instagram profile if you do it this way.

(4) Create YouTube Channel

- You won't be able to do this without a Google account. If you have an Android phone, then most likely you've already created a Gmail account to use the Google apps. If not, then simply go to Google.com and click "Sign In" and follow the steps to set up a new account.

- If you're logged into your Google account, then navigate to YouTube.com and find the link labelled "My Channel" which will then proceed to creating your channel. Look for the option for using a business or another name so you can create the channel in the name of your practice.

- Note: If this is an account that many members of the team will access, then it might be best to create a Google account with a generic email address like frontdesk@practicename.com or info@practicename.com so there's no exposure to personal data.

(5) Create Twitter Account

Step 2: FULLY COMPLETE each profile with as much information that you would like to share about yourself and your business.

It's one of those things where you say to yourself "Meh, I'll do it later," but I suggest that you do it right away. This is especially important for your business, which should be obvious, but I've seen many pages where even the phone number hasn't been added to the page. Make sure to fill out every single field that each platform offers, as that is valuable real estate to showcase your business. The personal profile counts as well. You want to be perceived as real and as human as possible so when people look you up, your profile should be complete.

Step 3: Source your Twitter Chats and Existing Facebook Groups.

In this step you want to source out existing Twitter chats and Facebook groups that you can join to showcase and share your knowledge and expertise.

Let's start with Twitter Chats. The most exhaustive list of Twitter Chats and their hashtags that I can find is at https://www.tweetreports.com/twitter-chat-schedule/ where there is over 100 health related chats. If you search this page we're sure that you can find something relevant. But this list doesn't have all the chats available. You can also perform a Google search with a topic of interest and include the keyword "twitter chat" and you will see even more to choose from. Although it may be hard to find chats that are regional, remember part of the plan is to boost your online credibility and author authority. Being active with these chats will help you with that. Now go research and list your top 5 twitter chats here:

1. _____

2. _____

3. _____

4. _____

5. _____

Next up, the existing Facebook groups. To unveil the most appropriate groups for your type of practice, simply type a keyword or topic into the search box when logged into Facebook, click "See all results for..." and then scroll down to the Groups section.

Alternatively, you can navigate on Facebook's left panel to the menu item "Groups." There should be a menu item at the top called "Discover." If you click that you should see a list of groups that your "friends" are members of, and even more importantly, a column for "Local" groups. You can also now filter based on categories like "Health and Fitness" which would probably be appropriate.

Click the "Join" button. Make sure you research the group by reading the description and fully understand what they're all about. You only want to join the groups that are the right fit for you. Also, many groups have rules for their engagement, so you'll have to adhere to these or you'll end up getting barred.

Now go research and list your top 5 Groups and list them here:

1. _____

2. _____

3. _____

4. _____

5. _____

Step 4: Create Your Facebook Group(s).

Annoyed that you can't say what you want to say in the other groups you've joined? Does the perfect topic for your practice not exist locally? Don't fret. It's time to make your own group! A place where you get to control the experience for your members.

Facebook groups can be public, closed, or even secret, so you'll have to choose what makes the most sense for your practice. I will suggest making a public group for now so you can easily fill it with people from your community; however, you can create a closed group so you can vet the members before they come in. A closed group gives you the added opportunity to charge a nominal fee to be part of it. A closed group is still searchable by the public who must ask to join. The next level is the secret group. For this group you must be in the know and invited to join. For health practitioners I would say to leave this out for marketing purposes. However, this would be a great option for supporting current patients or clients of yours.

Note only a personal profile can create a group. This means that your practice page entity can't create a group.

1) Choose the best category for your group based on the research you conducted on Day 1 & 2 and list it here:

   _____

2) Navigate to Groups from left menu pane of your Facebook Profile and click it. Then click the "Create Group" button at the top of the page.

3) Then you'll set your group name, can start adding people, and set the privacy level. Add a nice cover page image and make sure to name your group with your town, city, or region in the title. You want to encourage local people to join. You can direct the public to your group from your website, encourage your current patient/client base to think about friends or family who would benefit from the information, email your mailing list letting them know about the new group and encourage them to share, and probably the most effective would be to create YouTube videos and blogs around the topic with links to join your group. You

can even enhance it by giving them a free gift download if they join.

4) Encourage the members to engage by presenting challenges, health tutorials, Q&A's, Quizzes, and Polls. And don't forget to use Google Trends for free or pay for a service like http://buzzsumo.com to keep your content current and interesting. Remember the point of this group is to showcase your knowledge and expertise around a topic, condition, or pain point with the ultimate objective of genuinely helping the members. This type of nurturing translates into patients or clients coming to see you in person.

Step 5: Develop the format for your Practice Insta-story Day of the Week for Instagram.

You should have already created your Instagram business account in a previous step, so what we will be working on here is putting together a format for your weekly day-long Instagram story for your practice. The first thing that you will need to do is choose a day of the week to do the story. I recommend that you stick with the same day each week unless you have a special event. Reason being, that will help you and your team create a habit. For example, if Fridays are wonderful days in your practice where most patients and your team are excited and filled with energy, then that would be the perfect day to choose.

Practice Insta-story Day of the Week:

_____

Choose the elements of your story in the morning or pre-shift huddle. Review which team members will perform each task and which patients or clients you will ask. It's probably best to plan on approaching a few patients just in case some choose not to participate. Of course, it's not a problem if they all want to take part. Also, when writing your captions, think about current trends from your research on Day 1 to connect the story elements or run a common theme throughout. Although you can make a single example here, this task should be performed weekly so you can stay current. You can use some or all of the following throughout the day:

- Trending Topic: _____
  - o Staff picture with their positive quote or insight for the day
  - o Patient Testimonial: _____, _____,
  - o Video of the Waiting Room
  - o Staff Interview: Staff Member:_____
    Topic: _____
  - o Picture of health practitioner at work
  - o Health Practitioner Interview: Practitioner_____
    Topic: _____
  - o Pictures of patients
  - o Create fun Boomerangs (GIFs)

*Note: Don't forget to use filters to add a little fun to your story elements.

Step 6: Create 6 videos for your YouTube channel and optimize for search engine ranking.

There is an astonishing amount of content that is uploaded to YouTube every day. Stats show that there can be as much as 35 hours uploaded every single minute. That means there's a ton of content out there for people to sift through. However, the good news for you is that I would bet dollars to doughnuts that most of the other health practitioners in your area who are "competing" with you for new patients (for lack of a better way of saying it, as we know we're really all working together, right?) are not creating videos regularly, leaving this territory untapped. That doesn't mean you don't have to produce compelling videos, but that does mean that you can take advantage of this fact and use the platform to help you climb to the top of the searches even if your website is not there yet. This is what makes this step so important. Google lists videos from YouTube right within their search, so if you have a relevant video for a given search term, then it's possible for it to show up.

For example, you are a physiotherapist and you have a website. Your ideal patient is someone with shoulder pain. You have a page on your website dedicated to shoulder pain, but for your location, when someone searches shoulder pain, your page comes up on the 10th page. You then create a detailed explainer video on the same subject and post it to YouTube. If optimized correctly and views consistently grow, then it's possible that video of you can show up on first page ahead of your "competition."

1. *Write 6 video scripts.* Try to keep your videos between 2 and 3 minutes long, which would be about 500 words. You will be surprised how much information you can include in that time frame. For these videos, focus on giving value around your topic but don't forget to include how you help people as well. The best practice for filming is to make sure you are well lit, record with a microphone if possible and memorize the script if not able to wing it. If time is a factor, then you can set your recording device next to a computer monitor and use a free online teleprompter like http://www.easyprompter.com.

    The breakdown for writing your scripts can follow the same questions for writing your blog articles. Look back to the chapter on blogs to see those lists of questions.

Script Example:

Topic: Chocolate and Weight Loss

(Hold piece of chocolate in front of camera, then take a bite and start talking)

Hi, my name is [name] and I've been a weight loss and lifestyle coach for more than [#] years. I've witnessed thousands of people [including myself] struggle with their weight, so I know exactly how you feel. You may have a lowered self esteem, little to no energy, and you might even be scared that you're on the path to diabetes or heart disease, as your doctor keeps telling you that this is what your future holds if you don't make a change. The worst part is that if you're like most people I've met, then you're probably extremely frustrated and tired of conflicting information about what to eat or how to exercise. And further, you have a busy life; so trying to research or keep up with these programs is nearly impossible. And I don't blame you if you're frustrated. Nothing is worse then being ready to make a change mentally, yet having no clue how or where to start physically. You end up throwing your hands in the air and continue down the same path.

Two out of three people in North America are overweight and one third is considered obese which is a HUGE number. So you're not alone. Understanding the problem and taking action has to be your number one priority.

With years of experience in the industry, I've learned so much about understanding the problem and how we can achieve amazing results with an affordable solution. A solution that addresses the key factors like lack of nutrient-dense food, toxicity, and inaccessible healthy options. A solution that is so easy to follow and doesn't take away the foods that you love, like chocolate!

Chocolate has many health benefits, but we're not referring to Mars and Snickers here. Dark chocolate comes with the following health benefits and contains:

- Powerful antioxidants

- Nutrients like fibre, iron, magnesium, copper, potassium, and zinc

- Healthy fats

- Flavanols that may help lower blood pressure and possibly protection for your skin

In the end it all comes down to balance. If you don't over indulge and you stick to the right type of chocolate, then it SHOULD be a part of your nutrition plan. And that's good news because who doesn't love chocolate.

If you ever have any questions regarding my videos, then please feel free to comment below, and if you know anyone that would benefit from this information, then be sure to share it with them. Until next time, I'm [name], have an awesome day!

2. *Optimize your video visibility.* Your videos should be findable both within and outside of YouTube. As previously mentioned, videos often appear on the first page of Google. Do this right and you can springboard yourself to the top of the search even if your website pages are still way behind. To do this you'll want to make sure to set up your Title, Description, Tags, Category, thumbnail, subtitles, and closed captions for each video correctly. This information is referred to as your videos metadata.

a. Title – Under 60 characters, include your keyword(s) and make sure your title starts with them. You can create titles with a ":" as well to offer a subtitle portion to rephrase your keyword. Examples:
    i. Sciatica: Common Causes and Natural Solutions
    ii. Teeth Whitening: What You Should NOT Do for Whiter Teeth
    iii. Lean Muscle: Top 5 Foods for Sculpting Your Body

b. Description – Only 100 characters are shown without having the user click "Show More" so be sure to include your important links like your website/Facebook groups/Opt-in Landing Pages first. Write a detailed description of your video next, which you can do by refining your video transcript if not pasting in the whole thing. It's worth transcribing each video into text for use with things like this and adding subtitles to your video (if you're too busy to do this yourself, not a problem, there's plenty of people over at fiverr.com that would be happy to do it at an affordable rate. Just make sure they provide an .SRT file as well to use for your captions on the video). The description should be rich with your keywords and variations and most likely your video transcript would contain all those gems. At the bottom you will want to add links to all your other social platforms for your practice, which you can add to a default channel description to save you the time listing this common information.

c. Tags – Highlight your main keywords in your tags. Tag the most important keywords first and then include other associated keywords and long-tail versions (meaning keyword phrases).

d. Category – YouTube does not have a health related category so I would categorize under People and Blogs,

Education, or Science and Technology

e. Thumbnail – This is the first main image that the viewer will see when your video is listed on Google or YouTube search results. This can have a substantial impact on the amount of clicks and views you get. YouTube will automatically assign a thumbnail from a clip of your video, but we recommend that you upload a custom image instead. There are many great resources online for determining what the best images are to use, so take some time to look that up when setting up your video.

f. Subtitles and Captions – Yes these are helpful for viewers who are hearing impaired or in a place where audio isn't appropriate, but they also help to optimize your video in the search as another opportunity to highlight your keywords. We talked about your transcript earlier, so be sure to upload your transcript, but there is also the option to have YouTube transcribe your video automatically if you haven't already produced an SRT file to upload. However, it may require some fine-tuning to get it right.

g. Cards and End Screens – Cards are small, rectangular notifications that appear on your video to help with engagement throughout the video. If you make a reference to a book you've written for example, you can provide a link in that spot for your viewers. This enhances the viewer experience and we know Google loves user experience when ranking content. End screens allow you to extend your video for up to 20 seconds directing viewers on what to do next after the video is done. Promote your website, Facebook group, other social media links of yours, or other videos you've published. It's essential to add these to each of your videos to keep the continuum of your practice brand.

Step 7: Create content for your Personal Facebook Profile, Practice Facebook Page, and Instagram and load your scheduler.

A vital component of your social proof is the number of followers you have for your practice's main social media platforms. You won't be able to grow that following without producing content on a regular basis. This is where most health professionals groan because at a first glance it appears to be more work stacking on top of the never-ending to-do list, but it is important. With some planning, scheduling, re-purposing, and delegation, you can pepper all your accounts with regular content so that they look alive and attractive to follow. It's not just about flashing information; the real goal is to create a community of engagement. This method is part of your farming techniques for nurturing. Although platforms like Facebook restrict the number of people that will see your posts organically in their newsfeeds (without having to pay), there will be some level of an audience that will receive them, the page will be searchable on the search engines like Google, and if you're interacting within the social platforms, then it's common for people to follow up with your personal profile or pages. If they like what they see, then they may become a new friend or follower, which means they become a part of your farming community. Warming them up as a prospective patient or client, you can nurture them until they become an actual patient or client down the road. However, if your personal profiles or practice pages are empty, you greatly decrease the chances of building an audience.

In my experience working with hundreds of health professionals, the biggest challenge is simply getting content ready and distributed. That should be the obvious first step. Like patient or client care in your practice, if your profession promotes maintenance visits, some care is better than no care. As part of the social media content plan, something is better than nothing. Start by simply getting something up on a regular basis.

The next step is where most health professionals drop the ball as they forget what the whole point of the content is. We want to produce content that your current patient or client base will want to share with their non-patient or client friends. Then you can nurture all the new prospective patients or clients from a place of awareness to the place of conversion. This requires that you define your target patient or client. For some it may be everyone 18 or older. It's possible that others want to target children or families, while others prefer to help seniors primarily. This is all about getting to know your ideal audience in detail and understanding their pain points. The best way to do this is by creating a perfect patient or client avatar. Use the following template to write down the details so you can produce content that serves this person from awareness to conversion.

Here is an example of what not to do:

Patient or Client Avatar: Our perfect patient is one that has the money to afford our care and is in chronic pain. They are not looking for conventional care and are open to new ideas about their health.

This previous example lacks detail. You need to truly understand this person. The avatar should look something like this. Using an image is also very helpful. Let's assume that a psychologist is creating their perfect patient avatar:

Name: Sarah Parker

Gender: Female

Age: 47

Children: 2 (Boy 18, Female 15)

Location: San Diego, California

Occupation: Lawyer

Annual Income: $140,000/yr

Level of Education: Professional Degree

Highest Values:

Sarah is a hardworking individual who loves her career and her family. She spends most of her time working but enjoys reading books on politics in her spare time. She cares about her health although not physically active, but has an interest in mental health and personal development.

Challenges:

Sarah is having some problems with her marriage. She has been married for over 25 years and feels like the communication with her husband is lacking. They are fighting almost every day and it seems to her like her husband is not cooperating. She is concerned that the family unit is falling apart and her children are now starting to disrespect her as well. She is also like her husband in that she can procrastinate getting help, as her career is her highest value.

Possible Objections to Care:

Although she is not averse to seeking help, she feels like her husband will not participate in therapy. Her time is also limited which may interfere with continuity of care.

You should create at least 5 different avatars and develop content that entices each based on their values and challenges. For an example, we will walk you through the development of content for Sarah detailed above.

Using your avatar, you can determine the type of content you should deliver at the right time. This means that we need to think of the content to be delivered in stages.

- Newbie
- Nurture
- Convert

Note you can also use the same ideas for your closed Facebook group as well. Remember the idea there was also to further the awareness, nurture, and convert.

Newbie

For a psychologist to attract more people like Sarah, who at this stage would be a newbie, it would make sense to create something sharable so that your current following who want to help their friends or family would share it. This way you leverage your current following to attract new people. If it's valuable enough, then people like Sarah would want to join your community. The post could be something like this, which is a link to a blog on your website:

**Top 5 Ways to Have Your Spouse Agree to
Participate in Counselling**

If you know anyone struggling with their relationship, then
please share this article with them. These are proven techniques to help couples make that first step toward saving
their relationship.

Note don't forget that you can re-purpose these posts across your
social platforms. The above Facebook post can easily be converted
into a tweet or Instagram post.

If you have created 5 avatars as I suggested, then you should have
at least 2 original newbie related content pieces per avatar. Here
are some tips to help you complete this step:

a. Repurpose an old PowerPoint presentation into a slideshare
    online
b. Create a useful graphic of benefits of your care or specializa-
    tions
c. Write and post a case study about someone similar to the
    avatars
d. Develop a list of useful links

e. Create a quiz that would entice your avatars
f. Create a graphical "Top 10" list
g. Top 5 Tips Post
h. Develop a step-by-step, do-it-yourself guide
i. Interview a patient or client on video who has seen amazing changes to similar challenges of your avatars or who overcome similar objections to care

After this step is complete you should have 10 posts created. You should repurpose as many as possible to the other platforms as well.

Note You don't have to sit by your computer each day and post each of these individually. We highly recommend using a scheduling system built into your social platform. That way you can follow our planning schedule and create content months in advance. There is fantastic documentation on this online, so we won't go through how to set that up in this book.

Nurture

When creating your nurture content, try to answer the following questions for your ideal patient or client avatars:

What further information can you provide, whether it's your own or shared content, that can help the avatar understand more about your profession and specialties?

How can your services help with the challenges the avatars are facing?

What exactly is involved in the care you provide?

What proof do you have that demonstrates your care actually works?

Here is an example Facebook post to further the journey for Sarah:

Are you or your spouse nervous about starting couples therapy?

It's probably because you don't know what to expect. We realize it can be frightening for some to take the first step so here is some reassuring information that should calm the nerves:

1. The sessions are discreet and private.
2. Although the sessions can be awkward at first, we will always respect your boundaries.
3. We will be efficient. The goal is to mend the problems in the least amount of time so do not worry if you or your spouse have a busy schedule.
4. After overcoming emotional obstacles, you will finally feel some relief, which feels good!
5. 99 percent of our patients are grateful they attended and didn't continue to ignore the problem.

For nurture posts, you will need at least 10 per month as well. It's easy. Create one original post, like the one above, catering to each of the 5 avatars, then share 5 posts from other organizations applicable blogs, research, news articles, or other public access information that will help to further endorse the care you are providing.

Having the opportunity to show your knowledge and nurture a prospective patient or client is much better through engagement. Here are the top 10 ways you can help increase the engagement on your page:

1. Post a poll or a quiz
2. Ask a thought provoking question
3. Post on the fringe of controversy
4. Include posts of applicable current events or news

5. Post on trending applicable topics
6. Make an emotional connection
7. Ask your audience to share their stories
8. Host a contest
9. Add humor to your content
10. Ask people to engage

Convert

If you have done a good job through your newbie and nurture process, then you should have already had some potential patients contact you for an appointment, which is awesome! However, some people at this stage still require a gentle push. You will need at least 10 of these posts as well to complete your month schedule. The goal here is to have your nurtured audience, who is now confident that you can help them with their health challenges, take action and schedule an appointment if they haven't already. Whether you want to present an offer of discount or not, you still must effectively convey that they shouldn't wait any longer to take action at this stage.

You are free to do what you are comfortable with however, we believe that the most effective strategy is to present a monthly special, offer, or discount with a limitation of time or availability to encourage the action is taken immediately. We suggest creating a theme for each month of the year that you can connect your special, offer, or discount to. This will give it a purpose as opposed to appearing like you need more new patients or clients. Here are some examples of monthly themes you can follow:

1. January – New Year, New You
2. February – Heart Health
3. March – Caffeine Awareness
4. April – Autism Awareness
5. May – Allergies

6. June – The Truth About Cancer
7. July – Physical Fitness
8. August – Kids Month
9. September – Back to School
10. October – Workplace Wellness
11. November – Arthritis
12. December – Gift of Health

For example, if in December the theme is Gift of Health and you are a dentist, you can make an image post like this:

You can share the gift of oral health this Christmas. It can be anyone from a family member, co-worker, or friend who would benefit from our care. Simply add a comment with their name below and we will connect with them to activate this special gift! This is only valid for the first 20 people and ends December 24th so do not hesitate. If you're thinking of someone then let them know you're thinking of them this Christmas.

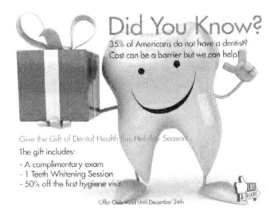

Step 8: Organically grow your following on Facebook.

If you follow the steps above and continue to do so each month, your page will organically grow a following. However, let's sum up all the tips you can do to ensure that you maximize the organic growth of your Facebook page.

1. Ask your current patients or clients in person to add you as a friend personally, or follow your page. This is fastest and easiest way to get started. With our experience, if they don't do it on the spot when you ask them, then most likely they won't remember to do it at all. Have a tablet ready and ask if they wouldn't mind doing so. Most would be more than happy to do it without any incentive. However, if you do offer something (like 50 percent off their visit, etc.) then you could easily convince them to leave a positive review online (which we will go over in the next chapter) as well as following you on all your social platforms.

2. Prepare content for other already successful pages or companies in your industry, which compliment the services you provide. Choose 6-8 pages and connect with them offering to develop relevant content for their page in exchange for credit. Watch your following soar!

3. Do promotional swaps with other services or products offered in your industry. If you can discover several businesses that will mutually benefit from working with you or accessing your audience then that opens a huge door for you. The drawback to this technique is that if you don't already have a large audience of 2000 or more, then anyone you approach might be reluctant as the benefit scale tips too far in your direction and not theirs.

4. Post, comment, interact on your practice's Facebook page

using your personal profile as well as making sure you share your posts from your Page on your personal profile. This greatly increases the exposure of your content and your page.

5. Don't forget about traffic on your website. Make sure your website has the appropriate amount of "like" boxes for all your blogs and that you have a "follow" box for your practice's page.

6. Aim for viral! You would be laughing all the way to the "follow" bank if any of your content goes viral. Buzzsumo.com has done some research and discovered that most shared content on the web has the following characteristics:

Emotional Element	Content Element	Topic Element	Format Element
Amusing	Images	Trending topic	List post
Surprising	Facts	(e.g. Zombies)	Quiz
Heart Warming	Charts	Health & fitness	Story
	Quotes	Cats & dogs	Curation
Beautiful	Video	Babies	Research insights
Inspiring	Interaction	Long life	
Warning		Love	Practical tips
Shocking			

7. Provide incentives to get more fans or followers. For example you can run a contest. The cost for entering to win the prize is to "like" or "follow" the page. For your current Facebook community, they can share the page to enter.

THE NEW PATIENT GENERATOR SETUP – DAY 6

(ONLINE REVIEWS)

Integral to Digital Marketing

Even though on the surface giving attention to positive online reviews might not seem like a digital marketing strategy, but for professionals it is a vital component. The nature of the business is based on a foundation of trust, respect, and reputation, and to maximize the number of prospective patients or clients taking that leap into your practice from the online space, you will need to have both your social proof boosted and your positive online reviews overwhelming.

Platforms for leaving a review are everywhere online. From Yelp, to ratemd.com, to Google Reviews, to Facebook, to the Better Business Bureau, if someone has something to say about you or your practice, they have a platform to deliver their message to the world. It has become a staple for credibility. The first time I encountered its power was way back when e-bay started. If I'm going to send money to a stranger, what's stopping them from keeping my money and not sending the product? I quickly learned how a bad review or rating could destroy an online business and realized right there. However, as the internet became the hub for information for all businesses on and off the internet, the review capabilities expanded to almost all businesses!

These reviews hold a powerful effect on how well you are perceived to a prospective patient or client, so they cannot be ignored. According to a survey by BrightLocal, 88 percent of consumers trust an online review as much as a personal recommendation. Think about that for a second. I will assume that your best new patients or clients are those that are referred to you from your existing patients or clients, and what that statistic means is that if you had a solid list of positive online reviews, then 88 percent of those that read them would walk into your practice as if they had a personal recommendation. This is worth your attention.

Note another benefit of having an ever-increasing number of positive reviews is that search engines, like the all mighty and powerful Google, will rank your website higher in the search.

By the end of this 14-day setup, you want to have at least 8 positive reviews online. We suggest that you have your current patients or clients review your services on Google so you get the maximum effect for improving your search ranking. The reviews can be as short or as long as they want; however, the more detail they provide, the more credible the review will be perceived and the more power it will have to encourage someone to make the decision to come to your practice.

Step 1 – Ensure you have set up all the information on your Google places for business account.

If you haven't done so already, start by creating your Google Places profile. You can search online for the steps required to do so. This will add your business to Google maps, allow you to add essential information about your business like the address, contact information, operating hours and the ability for people to leave reviews. The other review platforms I would leave for now and do later. Google is the most important.

Please note it is possible that people could be leaving reviews for you on the other platforms even though you didn't set up a profile. It's also possible that you will receive some negative reviews from time to time, even if you didn't do anything wrong! It can be very tough to get these removed, so the better strategy is to flood as many of the platforms with positive reviews, especially on Google.

Step 2 – Ask your current patients or clients to write a review.

It's as simple as that. Believe it or not, they want to help you! They know how important reviews are for your business, and they do want to see you become more successful if you provide an excellent service, of course, which I'm sure you do. However, asking them to write a review and expecting them to remember to do it when they get home is almost a plan that is surely to fail. The best strategy is to have a device ready on the fly, so they can do it on the spot. If you're finding that most are being reluctant to participate then you can think of some incentives for them to do it. Remember, each positive review could translate into thousands of dollars in revenue so it's worth it to do all that it takes to get them. Here is a template of questions you can provide for them to help get the creative juices flowing:

Patient/Client Review Questions

1. What was your life like before coming to see us?
2. What is your life like now?
3. What do you like best about being a patient or client in our practice?
4. Why would you recommend our services to your friends or family?

Step 3 – Set up an ongoing bonus structure for your staff for each review they cultivate.

This is a fantastic strategy to help maximize the number of reviews on an ongoing basis. Review solicitation should be a part of your practice processes, and setting up cash or gift bonuses for reviews staff members are responsible for obtaining is a fun way to keep the review train on the tracks.

Step 4 – Reply to your reviews.

If a patient or client leaves you a review, they love it when you follow up and acknowledge them. The best part is that you can provide additional insight about your services as long as you stay within your profession's privacy regulations.

THE NEW PATIENT GENERATOR SETUP – DAY 7, 8 & 9
(EMAIL MARKETING)

> *"66 percent of consumers have made a purchase online as a*
> *direct result of an email marketing message"*
> *– Direct Marketing Association*

Email Marketing Is Not Dead

Up until this point we've been blabbing about tweets and likes and posts and shares, but we haven't yet mentioned anything about what most professional digital marketers would say is the backbone – email marketing. The reason they feel it's so important? Almost all age groups and demographics have an affinity for their inbox. It is a sanctuary from the chaos of the web and social media, their very own private virtual fortress of solitude where they can be as excited to receive an electronic message as they are when a physical package arrives at their home. Think about how effective this digital marketing method could be with the right message, to the right person, delivered at the right time. That's where the magic happens. The problem is most people have no idea how to do it right and it takes some work to get it all set up so it's automated. Also, when creating the content, we tend to forget that we're in *their* place of solitude. A place they want to be free of sales pitches and advertisements, so if your messages scream either of those, even if they've asked to receive your emails (which permission is mandatory these days), then don't be surprised if you get slapped with the dreaded "unsubscribe" from many of the contacts on your list. Successful email campaigns use an accepted etiquette that we will show you in this chapter.

In my experience, most of the health professionals that we work with have very limited understanding of the email marketing processes, so it's probably best to start with the basics of an email campaign and then provide some examples you can build from. This way you can see the parts of a full campaign from the ground up and tweak as necessary to make it personal for yourself and your practice.

Email and the Prospective Patient/Client Journey

You can use email marketing for many objectives including:

- New patient or client acquisition
- Practice branding
- Increasing traffic on your blogs or website
- Engaging your audiences
- Direct sales of products
- Increasing your patient or client referrals
- Reactivating old patients or clients
- Strengthening the relationship with your existing patient or client base

In fact, you *should* be using it for all the above objectives to receive the full benefit of this powerful marketing tool. However, let's review the full marketing journey for a prospective patient or client all the way through from the beginning. I really like the explanation and detail provided by digitalmarketer.com who breaks down the marketing journey into the following sections:

1. **Create Awareness:** It's not that surprising that there are probably thousands of people in your community that need your services. They either know it, or they don't. By the end of the 14-day setup we will have awareness initiatives for both. Between the organic initiatives, we detailed earlier like blogging and your social media content or the paid traffic campaigns that we will discuss in the upcoming chapters, a key objective is to build awareness about you, your practice, and your services. In other words, your prospective patient or client either came across one of your blogs or articles online navigating through another website or possibly through a search engine like Google, or became a member of your private group on Facebook, or had some content shared with them from something you posted on your Facebook page or possibly an Instagram story or tweet from Twitter, or they saw a paid advertisement on Facebook or Google Ads. It is usually best to create awareness without asking them to subscribe to your mailing list right away, especially if they don't even know anything about you or your services. Spending some time educating is very helpful and then follow up by retargeting them in the future with the option to subscribe. However, you can try starting with campaigns for subscriptions to a cold audience and see how it works out. Every industry, topic, and audience is different, so it's always best to test.

2. **Subscribe:** The next step is adding this prospective patient or client to your email list. Typically, this is done by giving something of value for free in exchange for their email. Here are some examples of freebies you can create:

    a. Quiz
    b. E-report
    c. E-book
    d. Create a challenge, i.e., The 30 day Weight Loss Challenge

e. Template or worksheet
f. Automated webinar
g. Step-by-step guide
h. Audio training
i. Complimentary services

Each health industry is different so it's best to try each of these to split test which would be most effective. All the above have proven to work across most industries within and out of healthcare, so you can proceed with confidence that you should have success with many of them. If you're asking yourself how you can set these up, then you can easily develop amazing opt-in pages with an online service like clickfunnels.com and they even have a built-in emailing system as well which is win-win. We will detail more about this when get to the implementation section.

Building your email list this way allows you to have a disclaimer next to the opt-in button on the page that clears you with permission to email them in the future. Also, keep in mind what's going through the heads of your visitors. "Is there any real value here with this gift?" "Are they going to spam me to death?" "Are they going to blow up my inbox with messages?" "What other benefits are there if I give them my email?" "Will the emails I receive be of value?" Addressing these concerns at this stage will make a difference.

YES, YOU NEED PERMISSION! If you're thinking about buying an email list to get started, then DON'T! It may be cheap and it may be quick, but if you use those lists then that makes you a SPAMMER! You probably won't go to jail if you get caught, but most countries have regulations in place so that you could lose your privileges online which could harm your business. Not to mention that all you will probably do is annoy and frustrate people with your brand which would be counterproductive to your objective. Do it the right way.

---

3. **Engage:** Now that the prospective patient or client is part of your inner email circle it's time to build your relationship further by delivering value. You do so through the following:

   a. New subscriber welcome and delivered free digital gift
   b. Professional biography
   c. Links to your blogs or articles
   d. Notifications for upcoming webinars
   e. Surveys
   f. Announcements
   g. Contests
   h. Quizzes

Ask Your Subscribers to Whitelist Your Email: Deliverability of your emails is an important thing to consider. If you've prepared an A+ email campaign with all the fixings, yet the email service providers are sending all your messages to the junk box, then all your effort is literally being thrown into the trash. You can help ensure the successful deliverability of your messages by asking your subscribers to whitelist your email address. This essentially adds your email to their service marked as a friend. You should provide instructions on how to do so within the first email you send them which would be the welcome email. You can view a set of instructions for all the popular email clients here:

https://www.whatcounts.com/how-to-whitelist-emails/

---

4. **Convert:** As soon as the 4th day after they originally opted in, you should be ready to start including your call to action for your services. At this stage, these prospective patients or clients should be more likely to recognize their health challenge and the necessity for getting help. They should

know all about you and how much you care about them, have trust in you, and are ready to come in to see you. You can offer an incentive to come in, which we find works best, or simply stress the urgency of what happens if they ignore their health challenge.

5. **Ascend & Advocate:** It's time to share your mission and excite your audience to join. Encouraging them to lock arms with you to help as many people in your community end their health challenges too. These emails will help position you and your practice as a leader with a purpose of fighting for a cause. The benefits are two-fold. One, you will strengthen the retention of current patients or clients and, two, they will be excited to refer others to see you. Here are some examples of assets that can help ascend your audience and turn them into practice advocates:

   a. Relatable case studies
   b. White paper reports
   c. Current, exciting research or scientific developments

6. **Promote:** Now that you have an army of advocates for your mission and vision, it's time to ask for referrals. If you properly ascended your audience, then they are already thinking of people who need your help, but they will need a little gentle encouragement to help them take action. You can offer incentives for their efforts or even have a seasonal contest. The key here is to make it easy for them to provide referral information to you but also participate in the process of connecting you to them.

Email Campaigns 365 – Automated/Triggered Emails vs. Scheduled/ Manual Broadcasts

Automated/Triggered Emails

Throughout the year, you should be consistently emailing your list to keep your audience thinking about you and engaging as much as possible. Some of the emails that are sent will be initiated automatically when someone first subscribes or takes a specific action in social media or on a landing page or blog, and some of the emails will be scheduled or manually initiated broadcasts going out to everyone on your list for something like a seasonal or holiday promotion.

Although newsletters would fall into this category, we're not going to go into detail about those. It's possible your website service has an automated sequence for these anyway. But one of *the* most important automated or triggered email sequences for scheduling new patients is the initial emails sent to new subscribers. This will include what some digital marketers refer to as indoctrination and engagement.

Indoctrination

How likely do you think a prospective patient or client would take the leap to becoming an actual patient in your practice if your first 3 emails were something like this:

Email #1 Subject: Welcome John!

"Hi John, Thanks for joining our mailing list and downloading the free e-report. After reading through it, you'll know exactly why you should be receiving regular acupuncture treatments with us. Now it's time for you to become a patient. Check out this deal!"

Email #2 Subject: Did you take us up on our offer?

"Hi John, If you haven't taken us up on our offer, then what are you waiting for? If you don't do anything about your problem, then it's going to get worse. Don't hesitate, our offer ends tomorrow"

Email #3 Subject: Last chance!

"Hi John, Today is the deadline for our new patient offer. If you downloaded our report, then either you or someone you care about has a problem. This is the perfect time to take action so don't lose out. Take advantage of our offer now!"

Fine, you may get a few people that would take you up on your offer, but with this strategy you are really limiting yourself because now you're just being like every bad salesman out there. You're trying to build a relationship based on a bad sales pitch. More likely than having them take you up on your offer, you'll have them drop off your list in the first few days. This is why a proper indoctrination is so important.

You should view building relationships online like you would in person. If you're at a party and you have a product or service that you know could be helpful to someone there, you probably wouldn't get very far by running around and telling everyone to buy from you. On the other hand, if you walked around and introduced yourself, taking the time to explain who you are and what it is that you do before making an offer, then you would greatly increase your odds of success. In other words, for a solid, long-lasting relationship built on trust you better make a great first impression. You do that by making them feel welcomed and valued. Using a little humor also helps sometimes.

Another important piece of the indoctrination is letting them know what to expect and adding some action steps to take. That way they'll be looking out for your message when it comes in with the tidal wave of emails they get every day. You want to help create habits of engagement for future emails. If your audience isn't taking action by at least clicking the links you include in the email or possibly picking up the phone and calling you, then it's going to be hard to monetize, which realistically is the whole point. One step could be having your subscriber whitelist your email address, for which you can add instructions to do so. Another step could be having them like your Facebook page or follow you on other social media. The last step could be about letting them know about a special gift you'll be sending the following day. You should be perceived as grateful and appreciative with your emails so make sure that comes out in your writing.

Engagement

After you have successfully had your audience buy into you and have shown some of the value that you can provide, it's time to nurture your audience by having them consume more content right before you present your call to action for an appointment. These are the emails that are going to first attempt to convert your audience. These emails should reference positive previous actions the audience has completed, answers to key objections they might have, and present a clear call to action with proof of success for previous people who have taken action.

> *Note* The indoctrination and initial engagement email campaign are the only automated/triggered emails we are going to cover in this book. Also, we won't be going into very much detail with regards to scheduled/manual broadcasts.

Scheduled/Manual Broadcasts

To keep the communication alive, you should be scheduling or manually triggering broadcasts that go out to your whole audience base. However, it's important to segment your audience into three lists:

1. Active Patients/Clients
2. Inactive Patients/Clients
3. Prospective Patients/Clients

This way you can create promotions that will deliver the right message to the right person. You wouldn't want to pester existing patients or clients with emails about becoming a patient or client. You wouldn't want to send reactivation emails to your active or prospective patients or clients. Managing your lists can be a tedious job but extremely important. You can assign the task to your staff members to do a weekly or monthly clean up, create emails that let your audience segment themselves, or simply stay on top of it by including list management into your routine practice procedures.

Ascension, Segmentation, Reactivation

The talented team over at digitalmarketer.com also detail some other email campaigns that should be part of your yearlong plan. Although in the implementation section of this book I won't be giving any examples of these, I recommend learning as much as you can about them so you can stick them into your calendar. Remember how in the previous section we segmented the list into active, inactive, and prospective patients or clients? Well let's take the active list to start. These people are current, active patients or clients that are coming into your practice regularly. The goal with this list is to ascend them to a place where they possibly start buying products you provide or have them link arms with you on your mission to help as many people in your community as possible and therefore send you referrals. To accomplish this you would send messages that would be manually triggered.

Another campaign example would be a segmentation campaign. These emails are helpful to further categorize your list. Let's say you have a large number of people on your prospective patients or clients list. You want to further understand the symptoms they are faced with or health topics they have interest in. You can run a campaign with emails that have multiple links embedded for different topics that will give you the opportunity to further segment your lists across these topics. That way you can engineer your emails even deeper to further increase the chances of having them take action.

The last campaign type is reactivation. This can be used across two of your lists. You can run an email broadcast to your inactive patients giving them the opportunity to come back into your practice again. The other type of reactivation campaign that you can run is a broadcast to your prospective patients or clients list who have not interacted with your emails in a while. The purpose of these emails is to either encourage or incentivise them into engaging again or taking action in some way or removing them off your prospective list altogether.

Note To properly set up a segmentation campaign or a reactivation campaign to those that have not been engaging with your emails, then you would most likely have to use a marketing automation service as you will need functionality for tracking interactions.

CRM (Customer Relationship Manager) vs. Marketing Automation vs. Email Marketing System

You've probably heard these terms before and are possibly confused about what each one does, and further, which one to invest in.

Let's first break down the main functions of each of these systems so you can decide which would be the best for you based on your goals. You may use one or combine the benefits using multiple, so it all depends on how far down the rabbit hole you want to go. I understand it to be that Marketing Automation is the system that organizes, facilitates, and tracks your cold audience and then warming them up until they're hot, and then the CRM, which focuses on sales, takes over and tracks the sales as they become and continue to be a customer. Many systems blur the lines, and definitions vary, so I've tried my best to categorize the features in the table below. There are systems like Infusionsoft that have the best of both worlds; however, for the basic needs of your practice you probably won't need a system like this. The good news is that most health professionals can get away with using a simple email marketing system, which is easy to use and the least expensive. There are many products and services for each of these available, so please note this is a general overview of the differences of each:

	CRM	Marketing Automation	Email Marketing System
Sales Management	✓		
Marketing Management		✓	
Contact Management	✓ (Full feature)	✓ (Partial Feature)	✓ (Limited Feature)
Task Management	✓		
Workflow Management	✓	✓	

Sales Analytics and Reporting	✔		
Marketing Objective Analytics and Reporting		✔	
Email Automation	✔	✔	✔
Segmentation of prospects	✔	✔	
Purchase Tracking	✔		
Phone call Tracking	✔		
Social Media Integration	✔	✔	
Examples of service	ClickFunnels (Actionetics) Infusionsoft Salesforce	Infusionsoft Marketo Pardot	Aweber Mailchimp Constant Contact

As fancy as all of these look, more features aren't always the best way to go. They come with higher costs and provide many features that you probably won't use if you are not going beyond the training of this book. For the purposes of what we're setting up here, we recommend using Aweber or MailChimp for your emailing which will provide enough functionality to move your prospective patients or clients through indoctrination, engagement, and future manually triggered broadcasts. If you're already using ClickFunnels, however, for your landing page development, then you can look into upgrading to Actionetics for their easy integration email automation.

Step 1: Choose your platform.

Choosing the right platform for your email campaigns really comes down to understanding how much functionality you are actually going to need. For the purposes of this book we are going to cover the basics of email marketing which means we are simply focusing on email automation and broadcasting. This means you can probably get away with using a simple email marketing system like Aweber or MailChimp. I have become very familiar with Aweber, so I would recommend getting started there. It's easy to use and I have found the support team to be attentive and helpful. Plus they are consistently improving their system and adding new features. Many of the features that are yet to be added are provided by a third-party website called AW Pro Tools. Keeping it simple for now, we are only going to set up a 7-email sequence with the goal of turning as many prospective patients into actual patients as possible. We also want to map out some email broadcasts for special promotions that you'd like to run. Both initiatives only require a simple emailing system like Aweber.

I will try to speak generally within this chapter as you might not choose Aweber as your platform, which is fine. However, no matter which email marketing system you choose, it should have the same functionality. After creating your account, you will need to set up the following:

- An automated email sequence that is triggered when a new subscriber is added to your list (in Aweber, for example, it's called the Legacy Follow-up Series)

- Add the opt-in form on your website or landing page for people to be added to your list when signing up. Most services should have the code that you simply copy and paste to make it easy, but you may still need to stylize the form to match the look of your website, which your developer should be able to help you with. One advantage to using a complete package service like ClickFunnels is that they have these integrations built right in, and you can easily make the styling uniform.

- Generate traffic and entice your audience to opt-in. Some traffic will come organically as discussed in the previous chapters. However, some, and most likely more, will come from paid traffic, which we will discuss later.

To get started this will be enough, and the cost of these services is minimal. However, when you're ready to take your email marketing to the next level, we recommend exploring ClickFunnels and Actionetics. It's the easiest way to integrate your email marketing campaign and keep everything looking clean with the added benefit of saving money on website development costs. When you're ready for advanced ascension, segmentation, and reactivation email campaigns, then you'll have the functionality to do so. The best part is that you can track your users or potential patients' or clients' actions through the whole funnel process and create customized messages based on those actions.

What about Infusionsoft and Salesforce you ask? If you started to do any research into CRMs, then you probably came across one or both of these. They are both very powerful tools and are juggernauts in the digital marketing space; however, to the extent of what you would need a CRM to do for you as a health professional, these are too much. You can use something like Aweber or MailChimp for basic email marketing and ClickFunnels with Actionetics when you're ready for the next level.

Step 2: Write your Indoctrination and Engagement campaigns and set up email automation.

For my consulting clients, this is the hardest part. We can give examples until we're blue in the face and they still are slow out of the gate to get these done. Don't be slow to implement this, as it's one of the most important steps you can take to maximize your results with the New Patient Generator. The following is an example of the landing page and email sequence that we have used for two chiropractors practicing together who are consulting clients of mine. The potential patients opt-in for an e-report on numbness or tingling symptoms. Traffic to this page came primarily from paid Facebook advertising and Google AdWords. For these doctors we added an additional 15 new patients per month beyond what they were seeing from the other online marketing efforts. They are very happy clients.

Example Landing Page for Opt-in:

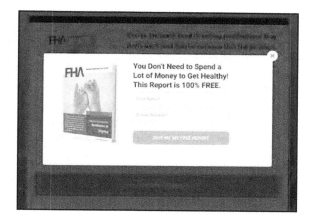

Note We added an extra step here to hide the form itself to help lower the bounce rate with the added value of a micro-agreement before filling out the form for their e-report.

Email #1

Subject: Welcome to Family Health Advocacy – FREE Natural Solutions for Numbness E-Report Download

Hey... We wanted to take a second to say hello and welcome you to Family Health Advocacy (FHA). We are Drs. Morgan and Casey Sinclair from Streetsville Chiropractic in Mississauga. We have teamed up with FHA, which is an online health advocacy group lead by doctors and health professionals providing resources and education on health matters that are important to you.

Congratulations on taking the first step to improving your health naturally by requesting your copy of our FREE E-book on Natural Solutions to Numbness or Tingling from our website. You can download the book by following this link:

DOWNLOAD MY FREE E-BOOK

Here's what you can expect from us...

As a subscriber of our mailing list you will receive emails every few days that contain information that we think will be important for you. The emails will be brief and provide a link to full articles from our website. The emails or articles may also include any promotions, specials, or upcoming events that we think you would benefit from. Our goal is to educate you on how to live a happy, healthy lifestyle while:

- living pain free
- taking less medication
- avoiding surgery when possible
- enjoying all the activities you love
- not wasting your time or money

Here's what to do next...

1. Whitelist our email address with your email service provider. If you don't know how to do this then follow the following instructions here.
2. Time to socialize. We have great natural health content on social media as well, so be sure to connect with us:

Facebook:
https://www.facebook.com/familyhealthadvocacy

Twitter:
https://twitter.com/familyhealthadv

Instagram:
https://www.instagram.com/family_health_advocacy

Yours in health,
Dr. Morgan Sinclair

Dr. Casey Sinclair

Part of the Family Health Advocacy Team
https://familyhealthadvocacy.com/

P.S. Stay tuned over the next few days...

We already have 3 or 4 amazing articles lined up for you that we know you're going see value in reading, so keeps your eyes open for them. We're excited to be part of your health journey.

Keep your eyes peeled. It's going to be great.

Email #2

Subject: As Promised... Your First Hand Picked Article

Hey... it's Drs. Morgan and Casey Sinclair... remember from yesterday?

In our last email we promised to send you articles that we thought would benefit you so we've handpicked this one that we think would be important for you to read.

However, we never really got a chance to introduce ourselves...

We are a brother and sister health team who were fortunate enough to be born into a chiropractic family with our father who is also a chiropractor. We have been living the chiropractic lifestyle our entire lives and we attribute a lot of our health and wellness, and the ability to do the things that we love, to chiropractic.

Growing up in a chiropractic clinic we were grateful to witness many daily miracles that occurred in our father's practice and we're so excited to continue to carry the torch for health and healing in Mississauga.

And now that we're old friends... here is a link to that article we promised you yesterday:

Click here to find out what NOT to do if you have numbness or tingling...

We think that you will appreciate the tips, as it's the same advice we give our patients. The article highlights the common pitfalls when trying to get rid of these irritating symptoms.

The article also outlines the EXACT things that we teach our patients to help empower them to overcome numbness or tingling symptoms naturally.

We suggest you go read it now because why wait? The article might contain the answers you've been looking for. Plus, we're going to send you another one tomorrow.

Yours in health,
Dr. Morgan Sinclair
Dr. Casey Sinclair

Part of The Family Health Advocacy Team

P.S. Well, we couldn't wait... there's so much important information on numbness and tingling to share that we're going to include another article here. And this is a perfect example of why you want to make sure that you read the emails right until the end.

Here you go:

How taking pills might actually be making you worse?

Tomorrow we have something very special for you. So watch out for the subject line:

"Top 5 Reasons You Can't Heal Your Pain"

https://familyhealthadvocacy.com
Sent care of Family Health Advocacy - A group lead by doctors and health professionals providing resources and education on global health matters. Be sure to check out our website for loads on information on Natural Health

Email #3

Subject: Top 5 Reasons You Can't Heal Your Pain

Drs. Morgan and Casey Sinclair here again. Are you ready for more? Today we have another eye-opening article that we know will interest you. So far, we've sent you the following...

Article #1: What You Should NOT Do if You Suffer From Numbness and Tingling — We held nothing back in this article. This is the exact type of information that we educate our patients on in our office.

Article #2: How Taking Pills May Actually Be Making You Worse — We understand that this one might have been tough to swallow but in order for your body to start healing you need to hear the truth.

... Along with a little introduction about who we are.

Did you read those? If not then you will want to do a quick search in your inbox for the subject line: "As Promised... Your First Hand Picked Article"

If you're caught up, then you really need to read this:

Top 5 Reasons Why You Can't Heal Your Pain

This is the most important article we've sent you, so even if you don't read anything else, then read this.

Remember that the only way out of pain is for your body to heal. Healing doesn't come in a bottle. This is key information that we give all of our patients when they first start care with us. This is without a doubt the most valuable piece of information that you're going to learn, so we know that you will enjoy the article.

Yours in health,
Dr. Morgan Sinclair
Dr. Casey Sinclair

Part of The Family Health Advocacy Team

P.S. Take 2 seconds to like us on Facebook and follow us on Twitter and Instagram:

Facebook:
https://www.facebook.com/familyhealthadvocacy

Twitter:
https://twitter.com/familyhealthadv

Instagram:

https://www.instagram.com/family_health_advocacy

https://familyhealthadvocacy.com

Sent care of Family Health Advocacy — A group lead by doctors and health professionals providing resources and education on global health matters. Be sure to check out our website for loads on information on Natural Health

---

Email #4

Subject: Natural Solution #9 From the Numbness/Tingling Report

Hi [firstname],

Did you get a chance to read the Family Health Advocacy report on natural solutions for numbness or tingling yet? If yes, was it helpful? If you haven't downloaded it yet, why not? Go back in your email and find it. Research studies show how natural solution #9 from the report is extremely effective for helping with these symptoms. And the best solution to your numbness and tingling symptoms will be one that is NATURAL and addresses the CAUSE. But...

... How much do you know about numbness and tingling?

Although there are many causes, most cases revolve around three contributing factors. Watch this video where we explain how your muscles play a role in your numbness or tingling:

LESSON #1 - How Muscles Contribute to Numbness or Tingling Symptoms

The more you understand your symptoms, the higher the chance that you'll be able to get rid of them. Go watch the video now. Take the time now to do something or you'll be forced to make time for your problems in the future.

Yours in health,
Dr. Morgan Sinclair
Dr. Casey Sinclair

P.S. We are located right in Streetsville, Mississauga. Check out our website at:

www.streetsvillechiropractic.com

P.S.S. If you haven't joined the Family Health Advocacy online community then please do...

If you haven't already then take 2 seconds to Like us on Facebook and Follow us on Twitter:

Facebook:
https://www.facebook.com/familyhealthadvocacy

Twitter:
https://twitter.com/familyhealthadv

Instagram:
https://www.instagram.com/family_health_advocacy

Email #5

Subject: [First name], how can we help?

Hi [First name]

A recent patient told us, "I really thought there was no hope for me. I've had numbness in my hands for years and everything I've tried doesn't work. I don't know what to do so I hope you can help." And the answer to her question, after we had the opportunity to do our special nerve examination, was yes!

As chiropractors we have extensive education in the areas of molecular nutrition, anatomy, pathology, and physiology which we combine with more education in neuroanatomy and neurology. Together with our clinical experience we have all the tools to give the answers you've been looking for.

Did you know..

... That bones and arthritis are contributing factors?

Watch this video where we explain how these play a role:

LESSON #2 - How Bones and Arthritis Contribute to Numbness or Tingling Symptoms

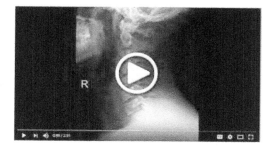

When was the last x-ray of your spine taken? Depending on your examination findings this could be an important step in determining what needs to be done to correct your problem. And that is something we can help with as we're professionally trained to take and analyze x-ray results. Make sure to watch the video above to learn more.

Yours in health,
Dr. Morgan Sinclair
Dr. Casey Sinclair

P.S. We are located right in Streetsville, Mississauga. Check out our website at:

www.streetsvillechiropractic.com

P.S.S. If you haven't joined the Family Health Advocacy online community then please do...

If you haven't already then take 2 seconds to Like us on Facebook and Follow us on Twitter:

Facebook:
https://www.facebook.com/familyhealthadvocacy

Twitter:
https://twitter.com/familyhealthadv

Instagram:
https://www.instagram.com/family_health_advocacy

Email #6

Subject: "I don't suffer from Numbness or Tingling Anymore!"

Hey [First name]

"I know how you feel. I've been there too."

Truer words have never been spoken. We interviewed an amazing woman; a mother, wife, sister and small business owner about her journey from suffering with numbness and tingling in her arms and legs that got so bad, she couldn't care for her baby by herself. We discussed her search for answers, reaching dead ends, and finding the solution that she says has transformed her life.

Jessica and her husband were thrilled when they found out she was expecting, and were overjoyed to welcome a baby girl into their lives. Labour and delivery was quite prolonged but Baby Maria was happy and healthy!

She began noticing a few new symptoms in her body that were unusual for her, but she ignored them, thinking that they would go away once her body fully recovered from giving birth.

Several months later, various symptoms were worsening, and she found it was difficult to hold her baby because of the numbness and tingling in her arms and hands. It was also difficult to make meals, take care of her home, and do all of the things she would normally do.

Jessica explained to us, "It got so bad that I couldn't pick up my baby anymore. I was so happy to have a baby but couldn't fully enjoy my time with her because I was struggling so badly with my own health. I always had to have someone stay with us to help me take care of Maria. It was then that I realized the numbness and tingling wasn't going to go away on its own. I needed some help."

Commonly, this type of symptom is caused by pressure on your nerves by spinal bones that have shifted out of alignment, a herniated disc, spinal degeneration or inflammation that irritates the spinal cord.

Ultimately, it's your NERVES that are affected. So this brings us to the last FREE video lesson:

LESSON #3 - How Nerves Are Affected With Numbness or Tingling Symptoms

Yours in health,
Dr. Morgan Sinclair
Dr. Casey Sinclair

P.S. We are located right in Streetsville, Mississauga. Check out our website at:

www.streetsvillechiropractic.com

P.S.S. If you haven't joined the Family Health Advocacy online community then please do...

If you haven't already then take 2 seconds to Like us on Facebook and Follow us on Twitter:

Facebook:
https://www.facebook.com/familyhealthadvocacy

Twitter:
https://twitter.com/familyhealthadv

Instagram:

https://www.instagram.com/family_health_advocacy

Email #7

Subject: [First name], have you resolved your numbness/tingling yet?

Hi [First name]

If you're STILL having any form of numbness or tingling in your arms, hands, legs or feet then please watch this video right now:

Yours in health,

Dr. Morgan Sinclair
Dr. Casey Sinclair

Step 3: Set up your email automation

Now that you have your 7-email sequence written, you've got to set them up on your email system. How you do this will depend on which platform you've decided to work with. The frequency at which you send the emails is important as well. If you send each one too spaced apart, then the subscriber might not remember you and forget that they opted in to receive emails from you. This could result in higher levels of unsubscribes or even worse, being marked as spam. If you send them too frequently, then they can get annoyed and unsubscribe or mark you as spam. Each industry is different, and the audiences might have different tolerance levels. We've found that for the healthcare industry this is the best timing for this initial 7-email sequence:

- Immediately after opt-in: Email #1
- Wait 1 day: Email #2
- Wait 1 day: Email #3
- Wait 1 day: Email #4
- Wait 1 day: Email #5
- Wait 2 days: Email #6
- Wait 2 days: Email #7

Step 4: Map Your Holiday and Seasonal Promotions

If all you did for your email marketing initiative was develop the 7-email sequence from the last step combined with all the other digital marketing elements detailed in this book, then you should easily be seeing at least 20-30 new patient leads per month if not more. However, there's still more that you can do, but we're leaving this step up to you.

Imagine for a second that there is a giant tree that has new patients attached to it like leaves. There are literally thousands of potential new patients attached to the branches of this thing. And imagine your total digital marketing effort would be like consistently shaking the tree with enough force so that these prospective patients start to fall and float to the ground. Your job then is to create as many nets as possible to try to catch as many potential patients as you can before they disappear. Or, if you want to think of it as creating one big net, that works too.

If you're really shooting for the moon, then you shouldn't stop at the 7-email sequence. You should create email broadcasts that each have an email sequence of their own throughout the year. This way you have regular touches of the people who are part of your segmented lists. Especially those that weren't ready to become a patient or client within the first 7 days after subscribing. Keep in mind that this doesn't include the regular e-newsletters that you should have going out. This is in addition to those. To save time you can just hire a service for your industry to do those regular e-newsletters as long as the content aligns with your practice values. The one thing they usually lack though is periodic calls to action. We recommend that you spend the time each month to develop a 3-5 email sequence for your 3 segmented lists. The following is a list of yearly events that you could plan these broadcasts for:

- Reactivations
- New Years
- Valentines
- March Break
- Easter
- Summer
- Back to School
- Halloween
- Thanksgiving
- Black Friday and Cyber Monday
- Christmas and Boxing Day

THE NEW PATIENT GENERATOR SETUP — DAY 10, 11 & 12
(PAID SOCIAL MEDIA ADVERTISING)

> *"Advertising works most effectively when it's in line with what people are already trying to do. And people are trying to communicate in a certain way on Facebook - they share information with their friends, they learn about what their friends are doing - so there's really a whole new opportunity for a new type of advertising model within that."*
> *— Mark Zuckerberg*

Foundation of Digital Marketing

Dr. Dan Brown owns and operates a wellness clinic in Scotland that provides services from various health professionals including chiropractic, personal training, and massage therapy. One of his goals was to increase the patient base for his two massage therapists and was hoping that there was a way to do that through marketing online. Good news for him, there was! The steps detailed in this chapter alone generated a whopping 24 patient requests in the last 8 days, which translates into a cost of £3.54 per request. Let's just say that he is a happy camper. The trick will be to sustain those results moving forward; so to do that, he will need to make sure that all the other elements of the new patient generator are put into motion, which he is working on now. We offer continued support through our private Facebook group and our online course and a common theme throughout is that if you want to see sustained results, then you must diversify your digital marketing initiatives. This is why we cover so much ground in this book. You can't be a one trick pony and expect to maximize your results.

If you were to have a crystal ball five years ago, see into my future and tell me that I would be helping health professionals with their digital marketing, I would say that you're crazy. With my background in computer programming and sciences I could see a possible connection and to be honest, even the idea of becoming a chiropractor one day would've sounded just as crazy. What a great feeling to graduate and finally get out into the great beyond of life to bring my talents to facilitate healing in the world. All that excitement was quickly attenuated by the reality that in private practice, new patients were not piling in through the front door. Man, I thought that college was the hardest part and if I could just get through then I would be cruising down easy street in a BMW. I learned a valuable lesson that challenges are endless, and success comes from understanding that fact while having the perseverance to continue and overcome them in pursuit of the dream. If I wanted to maximize the number of new patients that I saw each month, then I would have to learn how to market myself. Unfortunately, they didn't show me how to do that in college.

I absorbed as much from other doctors and mentors as I could. We would do health screenings in person at any event that would have us, we would do radio ads, newspaper, and dinner workshops. Most of the methods we did for over a decade would either cost an arm and a leg or I would bang my head against the wall because they consumed all my time. But, I did what I had to do. As life would have it, my priorities shifted to a family emergency and my time was limited. This meant that my marketing initiatives would have to change. Something that would be just as effective as everything else I was doing, yet something that would require less of my time. Then, a light bulb went off in my head! What about marketing through social media?

Over the last 15 years, digital marketing has become the foundation for marketing for businesses of all sizes. Interestingly, about four years ago, the spending of advertising online took the lead over traditional print newspaper, which I assume is attributing to its decline. I can understand why. You're now able to reach more people, target them with an unbelievable amount of detail, have them interact with your advertisements, they can see who else they know also enjoys the products or services, and all can be done for much less cost. When I first learned about this, I got so excited! This innovative marketing medium is going to allow everyone to get their message out there for a price that's affordable. This all was made possible by the social media platforms.

I knew that advertising through social media was where I wanted to focus. Taking what I had already learned marketing my practice through traditional means, I could easily try out some ideas but which social platform should I start with?

It doesn't take much research to learn that Facebook is the biggest player in digital marketing. I think that now, it's safe to say that it blows most of the other platforms out of the water, including the search juggernaut Google. Why? They have the most users with the most screen time and what I consider to be the best ad deliverability and interaction. This is why we are going to spend so much time diving into setting up your Facebook ad campaigns, which will be the golden nugget of your New Patient Generating System.

3 Types of Prospective Patients or Clients

Before we get into the step-by-step setup, let's explain a little further about all the things we want to achieve. In all health care industries, we've identified 3 types of prospective patients:

1. The prospective patient who knows they have a problem, yet they don't know that your profession has a solution
2. The prospective patient who knows they have a problem, they also know that your profession has a solution, however they don't know which professional to choose
3. The prospective patient who has a problem, but either doesn't recognize it or see it as a concern, and therefore isn't looking for help

The most effective digital marketing strategy would be one that contains initiatives that can address all three of these types of people. They can all be addressed right from your Facebook advertising however also supported by the other initiatives described in this book. Let's take number 1 and briefly describe their avatar. If they are aware that they have a problem and haven't done anything about it yet, then most likely they haven't had any luck in the past speaking to other health professionals, in some cases frustrated that they might have to live with their problems forever or potentially having to take some extreme measures which they don't want to do. They have absolutely no idea that you have the perfect solution for them that could possibly change their life. There could be thousands of these people in your community, and after you run your first series of Facebook ads and check the statistics of interest for your topic, then you will have no doubt that you have a massive pool of prospective patients or clients surrounding you. You simply need to deliver the right message to the right people at the right time. This group would be considered a cold audience. The best way to address these people is by running an awareness campaign (with no call to action) simply educating them about the condition or problem and how health professionals from your industry have helped. These campaigns can provide links to articles on your website, or you can make a single video or video series on a subject and simply try to get as many people in your community interacting as possible. If all you do is peak the interest of some people within this audience, then you've accomplished your goal at this stage. You can then retarget anyone who interacted in any way with follow up campaigns that either have them take advantage of an exclusive offer to come to your practice or you provide another free gift of information in the form of an e-book or e-report in exchange for their email address. That way you'll have another opportunity to nurture them further to ensure that they will take action.

What about person number 2 and person 3? Well the good news is that if you follow those procedures then you'll be catering to these groups as well. The well-rounded, most effective approach is one that will warm up a cold audience. All three of these types of prospective patients are cold so if you do the following then you'll be able to meet them all where they're at:

1. Educate about your profession
2. Educate about the conditions or problems that your profession can help with
3. Educate about the consequences of ignoring the problem
4. Educate about yourself
5. Educate about your practice
6. Nurture with information about how you can help
7. Provide success examples through stories and testimonials
8. Make it easy for them to come to your practice for their first visit

Although I don't recommend it, Facebook has the complete marketing platform to accomplish all the above objectives within itself. If you keep the traffic within Facebook only then you're losing out on the valuable traffic that could be travelling through your website. However, the cool part is that if you don't have a website that can be easily updated, or you haven't yet mastered a service like ClickFunnels, then you can do all you need right within the Facebook itself.

What I do recommend, however, is to go beyond Facebook. Use Facebook as a traffic generator in addition to its lead creation functionality. That way you can test your campaigns with greater detail. Each audience will respond differently to the next, so to maximize your results you should be testing how well your warm audience is converting on and off Facebook.

Anatomy of the Facebook Ad Campaign

Part of the confusion that causes limitations in performance when getting started with Facebook advertising comes down to not understanding how to organize your campaigns. You must choose the correct objective option from the start. Remember, health care professionals are not the only ones advertising on Facebook so there's a bunch of objectives listed there that will not suit you. I will explain the top 4 that you should use and what exactly you should use them for. However, let's first break down how each campaign is organized. You need to grasp this setup if you're going to properly measure your results and perform effective split testing of your ads and audiences. An improper campaign setup will cost you. I know from experience.

There are three levels to Facebook's campaign structure:

1. Campaign Level: This is the level where you set your campaign objective. We will discuss in this section as to which will be the best to use. You will need to know exactly

what your goal is for the campaign before selecting your option. Each campaign contains one or more ad sets and their corresponding ads. You can have multiple campaigns should you have multiple campaign objectives.

2. Ad Set Level: You can create multiple Ad sets for each campaign you create. Each Ad set will have its own defined audience, budget, schedule, bidding, and placement. Ad sets then each contain one or more ads.

3. Ad Level: This is the creative level containing the actual ads. To properly test the best ads for the best audiences with the best placement, you should have multiple ads active for multiple ad sets for each campaign created.

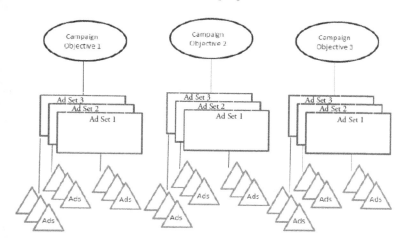

The Top 4 Facebook Ad Campaign Objectives for Health Care Providers

One of the first steps that you're going to take when you get to the implementation section is choosing the right campaign objective for the goal you have in mind. I thought it would be helpful to narrow down the best objectives for health practitioners, which will make it easier for you once you get started. Here are the 4 campaign objectives that I recommend you use:

o   TRAFFIC – This would be used as a cold audience objective. It's designed for your ads to reach as many people as possible for your ad spend that would be likely to click through to your website or landing page. You can also use this objective to pool an audience of people in your community who are interested in the topics or conditions you specialize in. Essentially, you would create an ad that links to an article on your website or landing page. Then using a Facebook tracking pixel, you can create an audience based on people that clicked the link or took action on that page. Over time, you will have successfully filtered the community down to people who are interested in the topics or conditions that you specialize in.

o   VIDEO VIEWS – This is similar to the above objective; however, the idea is to generate as many video views as possible. This is also a great cold audience objective where you can create videos on a variety of topics and try to have as many people in your community watch or engage with the video post as possible. This is extremely valuable. Think about it this way. If you're a massage therapist and you make a video explaining the top 5 causes of tight shoulders and neck, then you can pool all the people who have watched any length of the video which shows they are interested and then retarget those people with an offer for an appointment or opt-in for their email address. The best part is that right now this objective is quite cheap.

- o CONVERSIONS – This is the objective that you could use for your warm audience. You may be sending people to a landing page for opting in for an e-book or e-report. You may have an article on a topic that has an opt-in for an initial visit with you, or maybe you're doing something creative like a quiz or questionnaire that you want to them to engage with.

- o LEAD GENERATION – This is my favorite objective for new patient or client generation although it has its balance of downfalls as well. Facebook created this feature to allow you to have your audience opt-in for something right within Facebook. The benefit of this is that Facebook stores most of the contact information for each user, and for many fields, the opt-in form will automatically fill in. This means that with a couple clicks of the mouse they can sign up for something! The upside is also the downside, however. If it's too easy to sign up, then you get a higher number of false positives. I prefer the largest number of leads though, so nobody will slip through the cracks. You can get them on the phone and vet them to ensure they are the right patient or client for you. If you don't mind that extra step, then you will really enjoy the results this campaign objective will produce for you.

Targeting

I did a Facebook Live recently, talking about this subject on the page dedicated to our Done-For-You Facebook marketing service for Chiropractors called 3S Chiropractic Systems. The information I shared is something that all health care practitioners that want to advertise on Facebook should consider.

Targeting is one of the most powerful elements of Facebook's advertising. However, for health professionals who primarily service their local communities, targeting too much can really hurt your campaign. Remember, many Facebook marketers are giving advice on creating ads to millions of people, which is much different than a community or town of 10k, 50k or even 150k.

To be clear, I am not referring to the retargeting we've mentioned earlier, and I will be going into more detail about that in the next section. This is about setting your target parameters in the Ad Set level of your campaign where you have the ability to target based on the following criteria:

- Age
- Gender
- Language
- Interest
- Behaviors

I understand the excitement of narrowing your audience right down to the "perfect" patient, but a better strategy is to allow the prospective patients to target themselves. While running your campaigns to your cold audience, the best strategy is to keep the net for catching fish as big as possible. In other words, set very broad targeting parameters in an organized way. I'll explain what I mean.

For example, it's possible for a condition like Fibromyalgia to predominantly peak the interest of females over 40. However, it is possible that a female under 40 might need help with this condition, or even a male for that matter. If you create one Ad Set and target your already limited audience size to females over 40, then you've greatly decreased your pool and you'll 100 percent miss that one or two younger females and those few males as rare as they may be. I'm sure you'll want to see everyone possible. This is different, however, if you want to specialize in a demographic.

Like mothers or seniors. If that is the case, then you may restrict your audience to only include them and would probably be okay with the limited results. Keep in mind if your audience is 5 million people, then targeting becomes more important so you don't waste money advertising to a large group of uninterested people. That audience size, however, typically isn't the case for most health practitioners.

A better use of the targeting feature, however, is to split test the demographics, making multiple ad sets each with their own unique demographic parameter. You can make one for everyone under 30, and then one for 31 to 60, and then one for 61+. You're keeping your net large, covering everyone. However, now you've set it up so that you can use ad creatives that might be better suited for each demographic and even set different budgets for each. You can create different ad sets for all the criteria listed above as well.

Another idea that keeps presenting itself is targeting based on income. This idea, although it sounds glamourous, isn't all it's cracked up to be. Some Facebook marketers will say that it's the best way to single out the best patients for a private practice health practitioner, as the expense of your service can be a barrier for some. If we leave the argument aside that all prospective patients deserve your care, and that some low-income families or people actually turn into the best patients, I still don't believe this is a good strategy. Remember that income reporting on Facebook isn't fact. Facebook uses reported data and has partnerships with a bunch of data companies who share this information. They do this for not only income but other demographic data as well. Therefore, these numbers are not 100 percent accurate as there are too many places for error or miscalculation. So that brings us back to segmenting your audience with different demographics that crosses the broad spectrum. That way you increase your chances of collecting the patients or clients that you do want without having any missed, and at the same time have solid vetting procedures in place so that you don't end up with the feared "tire kickers." If I can add my opinion here, you should be vetting for people who value your care, not those that you think can afford it. Some might disagree with me and that's totally fine. This is my opinion, however.

Custom Audiences and Retargeting

Now that we covered targeting in the last section, let's discuss what retargeting is along with the feature of building custom audiences, as they go together. To keep this New Patient Generating machine running you must keep them moving through the system. You've spent all this money now on warming up your cold audience. You've had thousands of people click your ad or watch your video, so now what do you do? Just like a border collie rounding up cattle on a farm and steering them into a contained area, you will need to do the same for those people. You do that by retargeting. Building a custom audience based on the actions the people took with your cold audience ad. Now, rather than simply targeting based on the basic demographics, you've now created an audience of people in your community who have an immediate interest in exactly what you're sharing with them. This is a proven strategy to increase the numbers of conversions, or in your case, potential new patients or clients.

Note You can also create audiences of people who like your page or people who "look" like the people that like your page. I was helping a client named Dr. Gary L., who is a health professional in Ontario, with promoting a dinner marketing event. The concept is used across many professions both in and out of the health industry because it's so effective.

The basic idea is to host a free dinner for prospective patients or clients with the catch that there will be a short talk or workshop in exchange. We wanted to help him promote the event and fill all the spaces of the dinner with all prospective patients from his local community. If I remember correctly, the capacity for his dinner was 40 people so to help him reach capacity in a short time we decided to leverage our popular Facebook page Family Health Advocacy (FHA) to build a custom audience of people in his area that "look" like the people that follow that page. Gary is part of our FHA inner circle, which allows us to provide this opportunity for him. This creates an audience of people with an increased chance of success for his Facebook Ads promoting this type of event. After only 10 days of running the campaign, Gary had more than doubled his capacity and received 88 requests for his event. That is the power of customizing your audience with the right parameters!

Although we've had much success with cold audiences taking action within some professions we've worked with, you can't even compare the results to running your campaigns the way described above. It seems to be a known fact, because so many marketers say that people rarely buy the first time they encounter you or see your offer. Most take their time, compare information and check out your website and social proof a few times before making the decision to take action.

In case you are a visual person like me, here is an example of the prospective patient journey so far to tie it all together:

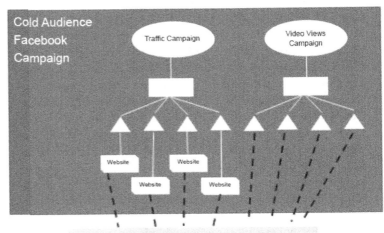

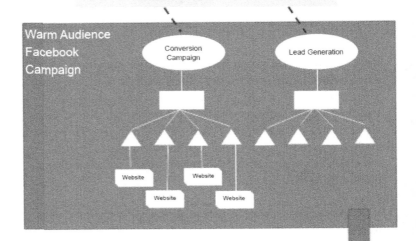

Split Testing

In a later chapter, we will discuss how to analyze your statistics and how to make decisions on which ads are working and which ones are not. The only way to maximize your results is to test. You should be testing everything:

- Variations of your ads
- Variations of your landing pages
- Variations of your emails

We manage clients all over the world, and yes, there can be differences between countries which makes sense, but we've also seen health professionals from the same industry in neighboring areas of the same city have differing results with roughly the same content. We learned quickly that the one trick pony for all health professionals everywhere will not work. Even the best marketers on the planet find it difficult to predict how an audience will respond. The best practice is to make variations of your content to see what works best. Facebook makes it easy to do that, ClickFunnels is fantastic for creating variations of your landing pages and most email marketing systems should be straightforward when trying to test varying emails for your sequence campaigns. For this section, however, we will just discuss Facebook ads.

As mentioned earlier, I will cover metrics and statistics in greater detail in an upcoming chapter, however, in a nutshell your concern for any Facebook ad will be about maximizing the number of people that see the ads (aka Reach) for the least amount of money. If the objective is leads, then you'll probably also be concerned with how much you're spending per lead. It's a numbers game. So, the more you reach per day, then the more likely you will land a lead. Facebook offers a few ways you can pay for your advertising exposure. The easiest would be simply setting your daily ad spend limit. The challenge, however, is that there are factors that determine how much exposure you'll get for your money. Facebook loves people who don't know what they're doing and tends to charge them more. Therefore, you'll want to get it right. This can be done through split testing.

You want to make sure you're getting a maximum Reach on your daily ad spend limit. And to do that, you need to understand how Facebook's ad bidding system works. If all this stuff seems like a lot of work and it's too detailed and you just want new patients in the door, that's fine. You just might have to pay more per patient, though, if you omit this part.

Essentially everyone out in Facebook land that is advertising to the same audience is bidding on advertising space like an auction. Depending on certain factors for your ad, Facebook might charge you way more than the next advertiser to reach the same amount of people. Why? Because Facebook also cares about their user's experience. Now you're probably wondering what those factors are? You may have heard other colleagues or advertisers talk about Facebook's Ad Relevance score as being important. This is true. Relevance is a rating that Facebook gives your ad on how relevant it is for your target audience. It is made up of a bunch of factors itself and only part of how Facebook chooses a winning bid for an ad.

The bids are won based on something called Total Value which is calculated by taking the actual bid price (which I typically automate) multiplied by Facebook's estimation of how well the audience will take action with your ad and those figures are added to factor for user value. This includes relevance, which is determined by expected interactions and actual ones like clicks, shares, etc.

Wow, what a mouthful! Are you ready to run for the hills and never look back? Well don't fret. In a nutshell, it means that if you have an ad that doesn't offer a great user experience, doesn't engage, or has much more negative feedback than positive, then

Facebook will simply charge you more. Which means if you keep a static daily budget, then you will reach less people per day, and therefore less leads most likely, if that's your objective. Content that encourages likes or shares is essential. The problem is figuring what content will do just that and which will flop. That's where split testing comes in handy. You create a bunch of ads that you think will win over your audience, and cut off the ones that aren't performing or costing you more. In the step-by-step section I will show the elements of the ads to focus on for split testing purposes.

Split Testing Tools

Facebook Dynamic Creative – You can find this tool in the power editor of your Facebook ads account. For the conversions, app installs, and website traffic campaign objectives then you will have this tool available to help automatically create multiple combinations from all your ad creatives. The tool will find the best combos of images, videos, titles, descriptions, buttons and more and develop a variety of ads while pushing the best ones forward.

Hootsuite AdEspresso – I consider this tool to be the ultimate for split testing. You can create hundreds of ads in minutes testing both demographic variations as well as multiple ad creative combinations. They have built in features for creating, analyzing, and optimizing your campaigns that is so easy. They boast that you can save up to 70 percent of the manual work needed to set up effective campaigns while at the same time improving the performance up to 40 percent.

The Other Social Platforms and Why Have I Left Them Out

So, what about Instagram, Twitter, YouTube, LinkedIn, and Pinterest? Are they any good for running paid advertisements on their platforms? That is a great question. Let's start with Instagram. This platform is owned by Facebook and most of the campaigns that you will run will allow you to link an Instagram page. This will automatically increase your reach to include the Instagram audience as well. This can be great as you'll receive more exposure, but something to keep in mind is that Instagram doesn't have as wide of an audience age demographic as Facebook, so including the Instagram network could add a larger number of younger people to your ads audience.

Pinterest has a large user base, which is good news for digital marketers however, like Instagram, the demographic does not span as broad as Facebook. The users are primarily female with the majority under 35. If that's your target audience then great, you might be able to harness this audience to your advantage, but for now I would recommend that you save your money and invest it all into Facebook, where most of the Pinterest audience is anyway.

Twitter, I would ignore altogether for paid advertisements as a health practitioner. The advertising platform is not as advanced as Facebook, and they seem to continue to struggle to grow their advertisers' base. This means something. We haven't had as much luck using Twitter and that doesn't mean there may not be some benefit, but as part of the New Patient Generator system we're building, for paid advertising, Twitter is left out of the plan.

LinkedIn is an amazing platform for business networking. It is not, however, the holy grail for new patients or clients. If you're looking for a new staff member, then it's possible LinkedIn could serve you, but if new patients or clients are what you're after then ignore this platform for paid advertising.

YouTube on the other hand can be a powerful advertising tool for your practice. One thing that I've learned, however, is that it's a difficult platform to master, especially for incorporating an effective call to action. For the purposes of this book we have left it out of the equation. But this could be a great topic for a webinar so keep connected to us online as maybe I will host something on this topic in the future.

Step 1: Set Up Facebook Business Manager.

You can set up an ad account as a personal profile or you can create a business account. I recommend using the business manager as you will have more control over your ad accounts. You will have the ability to create multiple accounts, so you can split payments across multiple credit cards, which may come in handy. With the business manager you can assign other people varying levels of access to any of the accounts that you create. For example, we have a client in Scotland who runs his practice ads through one account, which he has assigned us access to manage the ads for him, but he also has another business helping health professionals find jobs in their industry. He wanted to keep the charges for each ad account separate and with the business manager that was possible. This is the first step we recommend you complete.

Step 2: Set Up a Facebook Pixel for your Ad Account.

When Facebook first introduced the pixel concept there was a buzz surrounded by a little mystery. Maybe because it sounds like something that comes straight out of a fantasy movie. If any element of your prospective patient or clients marketing journey exists on your website or landing pages (external to Facebook), then properly utilizing the Facebook pixel is essential because it makes your marketing easier and more effective. However, like Facebook advertising in general, the pixel can be equally confusing if you want to push the limits of its functionality. In a nutshell, the pixel concept isn't unique to Facebook only. They are common across most advertising platforms. Facebook describes the pixel as an "analytics tool used to measure the effectiveness of your advertising by understanding the actions people take on your website." The main benefits are having an ability to show your ads to the right people, create new audiences from people landing on your webpages through the web, and unlock advanced tools within Facebook marketing. You can track each event at every step of a prospective patients or client's journey, which allows you to very specifically retarget them based on their actions.

For example, if you have built a landing page that has a free download to an e-report on the top 5 foods to avoid that discolor your teeth, and you want to build an audience of people who have downloaded the report so you can retarget them with a follow-up video within Facebook on teeth whitening that has an opt-in lead form for an appointment, then you can accomplish this with the Facebook pixel.

You can also set a separate pixel for each account that you create within the business manager. If you did set up a business account, then you will want to navigate through to the Pixels menu item, which is found under the Assets category. The main view will show you an overview of all your accounts, or you can select the account from the dropdown menu. To set up the pixel you need to install the code. For simply tracking clicks to the website, the code installation isn't very difficult. They have options for easy integration to multiple web platforms, services like ClickFunnels and WordPress have instructions on how to install your pixel code. It can be more challenging to install the code for pixel events so you might want to get some help installing those elements of code. We do recommend that you install the general code plus every single action someone can take on your website or landing page to receive the full benefit from this feature.

Step 3: Create Your Cold Audience Facebook Ads Campaign.

Now it's time for the guts of the New Patient Generating machine – Addressing the cold audience first with Facebook ads. This might be the first time these prospective patients or clients hear of you and further learn how you might be able to help them with their health challenges. We will use this step to help determine the most popular topics surrounding your profession in your area. Good news! If you completed the blog steps, then you already have published 10 blog articles. That will be more than enough for you to show your knowledge. However, I recommend that you create a video introducing yourself as well and showing your heart and vision as a health practitioner. Maybe even sharing some stories in practice or full disclosure from your life history to show that you're human. Remember, the whole point of this stage is to create ads that are simply educating with no call to action. As the ads run, we are collecting information of the interested people, which we will retarget, creating a warm audience for the next level of Facebook ads.

When creating the ads, remember to use the traffic or video views campaign objective. This will allow you to reach the most people in your community. The only targeting applied at this stage should be location. You will want to set the radius as wide as you think people will travel to your practice. Reminder, this is set at the Ad Set level of your campaign. The budget you set should be determined by the number of ad topics in your Ad set. As a general rule of thumb, for each ad topic I would use a budget of $5/day, so if you have 10 ad topics then you will need to set budget of $50/day to give Facebook enough to play with and test all the ads. You may want to try out some varying ad creatives for each topic, which is fine, and although that means you'll end up with more ads, you can still stick to the $5/day/topic rule and get away with it for split testing.

Here are some examples of ads for your cold audience campaign:

Video Views

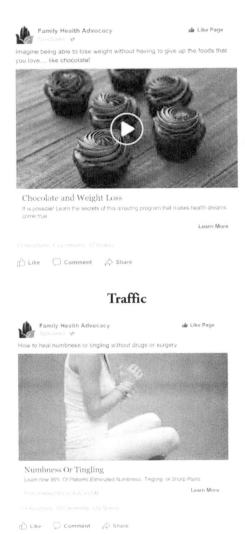

Family Health Advocacy
Sponsored

Imagine being able to lose weight without having to give up the foods that you love.... like chocolate!

Chocolate and Weight Loss
It is possible! Learn the secrets of this amazing program that makes health dreams come true.

Learn More

Like   Comment   Share

Traffic

Family Health Advocacy
Sponsored

How to heal numbness or tingling without drugs or surgery

Numbness Or Tingling
Learn how 85% Of Patients Eliminated Numbness, Tingling, or Sharp Pains

Learn More

Like   Comment   Share

Step 4: Create Your Lead Magnet.

One of the objectives with the new patient generation process is to build an email list. It's a powerful, cost effective way to communicate. At this point you should have created your email sequence which will help to convert prospective patients or clients into actual ones. However, you'll need to obtain their email address to start that process. The best way that we've found to do this is to offer an e-book, which I will provide an example of here for you. But in the following list are other ideas you can use for obtaining email addresses:

- How-to or Step-by-step Guides
- Top # List, Top # Mistakes Report
- Online Assessment or Test
- Quiz or Survey
- Template Library
- E-book
- Online course
- Cheat sheet
- Video Training Series

In the previous chapter I gave an example of a landing page for an e-book or e-report download, but you'll want to try as many variations of the pages as possible to see which ones convert the best.

If you choose to do an e-book or report, then it may take some time. Other options above might be quicker to produce, but remember, the more valuable the lead magnet, the more likely someone will exchange their email address for it. If you are going to produce a guide or report, then don't worry about the creative design. There is a great tool that you can use that will convert your text automatically into a well-designed e-book or report with the click of a button. Check out https://www.canva.com.

The following is an example of an e-report that we developed for general chiropractors running promotional opt-ins from our Family Health Advocacy website. However, if you're going to create one for yourself, then I recommend you add a little bio about yourself and practice and possibly some testimonials as well:

It's important to understand that the following information is intended only as a guide to help you understand more about your symptoms and to provide some tactful natural solutions to headaches or migraines. Please be advised that this is not a suitable substitution for seeking prudent advice or a personalized evaluation from a certified health professional.

Top 7 Natural Solutions For **Headaches or Migraines**

PAGE 1

familyhealthadvocacy.com

COLIN SWALA

TOP 7 NATURAL SOLUTIONS FOR HEADACHES OR MIGRAINES

DISCLAIMER CONTINUED....

Although headaches can vary in severity from mild to disabling, the vast majority of headaches do not require a trip to the emergency. However, the presence of the following should be evaluated by a doctor. Headache "red flags" include:

- Severe headache described as the worst headache ever experienced before that arises to that level within minutes. This should be treated very seriously and a trip to the emergency should be considered

- Constant headache present in the same location of the head without relocating or easing up

- Headaches with associated fever, chills, weight loss, night sweats

- Headaches with severe neck pain and sensitivity to light

- Headaches with neurologic symptoms. Weakness, numbness or tingling, or visual disturbances

- Headaches associated with any of the following: Sudden numbness or weakness of the face, arm or leg, especially on one side of the body, confusion, issues with speaking, walking trouble, dizziness or loss of balance.

It is also important to recognize that there are several reasons why one may experience a headache or migraine. Due to the array of causes and variations of their effects, it is important that you exercise due diligence while determining a diagnosis. Be sure to seek appropriate medical advice and care whenever necessary or in the event that you are unsure about the severity or source of the symptoms you are experiencing.

> My head is pounding. I wish I could just remove my head.

PAGE 2

152

TYPES OF HEADACHES — Primary vs. Secondary

How you describe your headache can help your doctor or health professional determine its cause and the appropriate course of action. As mentioned in the disclaimer, most headaches aren't the result of a serious illness, but it's important to note that some may result from a condition that is life-threatening and requires emergency care. Headaches are generally categorized as either PRIMARY or SECONDARY.

Primary

Although a sign of some level of dis-ease with an underlaying cause, primary headaches generally are not associated other medically diagnosed diseases. They are caused by problems, hyper sensitivity or overactive structures in your head that leads to pain. Any level of dis-ease you experience should be taken seriously however.

Physical pressure on nerves or blood vessels, muscles in your head or joints in your neck, and even chemicals from toxins or foods can play a role in this category of headaches.

Here are some examples of PRIMARY headaches:

- Cluster headache
- Migraine (with and without aura)
- Tension headache

Secondary

A secondary headache is a symptom of a diagnosed underlaying disease. Here are a few:

- Acute sinusitis
- Blood clot / Stroke

These headaches are controlling my life. I'm tired of taking medications which don't even help. And nobody really understands what I'm going through.

https://familyhealthadvocacy.com

PAGE 3

153

TOP 7 NATURAL SOLUTIONS FOR HEADACHES OR MIGRAINES

TYPES OF HEADACHES — Primary vs. Secondary — Cont....

- Brain aneurysm
- Brain tumor
- Concussion
- High blood pressure (hypertension)
- Medications
- Meningitis
- Overuse of pain medication
- Trigeminal neuralgia
- Thunderclap headaches

"I feel like my head is in a vice."

WHAT CAUSES COMMON HEADACHES AND MIGRAINES?

No question... if you are having headaches then something is wrong. Recurring headaches are not normal and remember pain is your body's warning signal that something is wrong. Your top priority has to be finding out the cause and fixing it.

All causes including nutritional, emotional, and physical should be explored but medical science shows that many of the common headaches are caused by damaged structures around the neck which can impact the nerves that go up into the head.

Poor posture from working daily at a computer or a repetitive work-related task or a car accident from years ago or sports injury. These situations may result in pressure on your nerves from shifts or misalignments of your spine, spinal degeneration or arthritis, or herniated discs. Those conditions will cause

https://familyhealthadvocacy.com

154

TOP 7 NATURAL SOLUTIONS FOR HEADACHES OR MIGRAINES

WHAT CAUSES NUMBNESS AND TINGLING? Cont...

Inflammation as well adding to further nerve irritation.

HOW TO PROPERLY IDENTIFY THE CAUSE OF YOUR HEADACHES OR MIGRAINES?

Seeking professional assistance for diagnosing the cause of your symptoms is strongly recommended. Your health professional will take a thorough history which will provide clues as to the nature of your condition. It is crucial to indicate any and all symptoms you have been experiencing regardless of whether you think they are related or not. Be sure to bring with you a list of all medications and supplements you are taking (prescribed or over the counter) and be prepared to let the health professional know of any previous care you may have received.

After reviewing the information and performing a physical exam, your health professional may require additional testing such as blood tests, electrolyte level testing, thyroid function testing, toxicology screening, nerve conduction studies. If necessary, requests may include imaging tests such as X-rays to have a look at the spine for further diagnostic insight. These will all be important tools in determining the diagnosis of your condition. After this step has been complete, he/she will then be able to make their recommendations and discuss various avenues of care or remedies to help correct address the cause.

> " It is important to address the cause of the symptom rather than merely alleviating the symptom itself. "

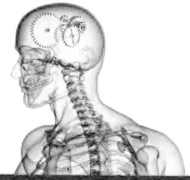

FHA https://familyhealthadvocacy.com

TOP 7 NATURAL SOLUTIONS FOR HEADACHES OR MIGRAINES

HOW TO PROPERLY IDENTIFY THE CAUSE OF YOUR HEADACHES OR
MIGRAINES? Cont...

"Remember" your goal for addressing any symptom you're experiencing
should be to identify the cause and correct it rather than merely relief of
the symptom alone.

TOP 7 NATURAL REMEDIES FOR HEADACHES OR MIGRAINES

1. CHIROPRACTIC CARE

Chiropractors are trained professionals who can identify causes of
headaches related to the spine. If it is detected that the spinal joints
and/or nerves are affected by shifts or misalignments then a chiropractor has the tools to help. By removing pressure with chiropractic techniques, this allows the body to function normally.

Research also shows that chiropractic is affective for helping with headaches and without almost any side effects when compared to medications. Here are a few studies:

The Bohne Study: https://www.ncbi.nlm.nih.gov/pubmed/7790794?
dopt=Abstract

> "
>
> My eyes hurt and I
> feel so drowsy from
> the medications.
>
> "

TOP 7 NATURAL REMEDIES FOR HEADACHES OR MIGRAINES

1. Chiropractic Care Cont...

The Duke Study - http://www.dynamicchiropractic.com/mpacms/dc/article.php?id=17938

2. Exercise

Even a quick workout may be able to stop your headache from progressing as exercise is known to trigger the release of endorphins which interact with the receptors in your brain that reduce your perception of pain.

You can choose something simple like low-impact stationary bike riding, swimming and even walking. Make sure to workout regularly. According to the American Headache Society:

"Regular exercise can reduce the frequency and intensity of headaches and migraines. When one exercises, the body releases endorphins, which are the body's natural painkillers.

3. Herbal Remedies

Headaches occur in people all around the world and in many countries people have used herbs traditionally to treat headaches. For example, a combination of feverfew and ginger helped to relieve migraine pain according to research published in the journal Headache.

You can try making tea with fresh ginger in water (or even chewing directly on a piece of peeled ginger or ginger candy from the natural foods store). Also, Rhodiola has been known to relieve headaches.

> Research supports chiropractic as effective treatment for headaches without as many side effects when compared to medication.

https://familyhealthadvocacy.com

TOP 7 NATURAL SOLUTIONS FOR HEADACHES OR MIGRAINES

TOP 7 NATURAL REMEDIES FOR HEADACHES OR MIGRAINES

3. Herbal Remedies *Cont...*

Rhodiola is helpful for tension type headaches, according to herbalists it increases levels of serotonin and therefore makes you feel good.

Coriander is also known to exhibit pain-relief for headaches. Here is a simple way to make a coriander tea:

Start by boiling water and then add a spoonful of coriander seeds. Let it boil for 3 minutes until you can smell the coriander fragrance. Then simply add in your favorite tea to the water.

4. Essential Oils

Essential oils are concentrated compounds from flowers and plants that are biologically active and volatile. They can provide large therapeutic benefits with the use of very small amounts.

You should consult with a professional first to understand the best use for your headaches or migraines. Essential oils can be administered at home or with the help of a professional the following ways:

Indirect inhalation with the use of a room diffuser or placing drops or sprays in the air

Direct inhalation with an individual inhaler with drops mixed with water (popular for sinus headaches)

Aromatherapy massage. Oils are diluted in another carrier oil and then massaged into your skin by a therapist or by yourself

Direct application to your skin with a roller or combining them with lotion. You can also mix the oils into your bath water and apply that way.

Coriander is also known to exhibit pain-relief for headaches.

https://familyhealthadvocacy.com

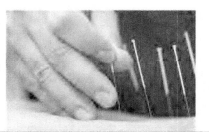

TOP 7 NATURAL SOLUTIONS FOR HEADACHES OR MIGRAINES

TOP 7 NATURAL REMEDIES FOR HEADACHES OR MIGRAINES

5. Acupuncture

Several studies have shown that Acupuncture can provide similar long-term results as medications minus the side effects.

Acupuncture uses the insertion of fine needles into specific points on the body which can be followed by gentle stimulation of the needles that can be mechanical or electrical. It's believed to work by increasing blood flow in the tissues as small vessels around the needle expand. While actions designed to increase circulation are generally an excellent treatment for pain including most headaches however it is believed that migraines are associated with dilation of blood vessels in the head and by stimulating the vessels further may cause a worsening of the symptoms. That doesn't mean that Acupuncture can't be used for migraines it just means that a special approach is needed that involves avoiding certain points on the body. A trained acupuncturist would know exactly what to do to help with your headaches and even migraines.

6. Stretching

As some headaches can arise from issues with the neck, here are 4 simple stretches designed to improve active range of motion and therefore help alleviate headache symptoms.

Chin Tuck Stretch

Bend your head forwards guiding your chin towards your chest. When you start to feel a pulling or stretch at the back of the neck then stop and hold this position for

> *Several studies have shown that Acupuncture can provide similar long-term results as medications minus the side effects.*

https://familyhealthadvocacy.com

TOP 7 NATURAL SOLUTIONS FOR HEADACHES OR MIGRAINES

TOP 7 NATURAL REMEDIES FOR HEADACHES OR MIGRAINES

6. Stretching Cont...

20 seconds and repeat three or four times.

Cervical Extensor Stretch

It's also important to stretch the muscles at the base of the skull which are commonly tight for most people. Bend the head forwards and turn it roughly 20-30 degrees to the left side.

Then use the right hand to stretch the head forwards. To feel the stretch underneath your fingers hold your hand at the base of your skull

Hold for 5-10 seconds and repeat 5 times.

Lateral Flexion Stretch

Sit on your left hand, with your right hand extend over your head and touch left ear, then pull your head right – you will feel a stretch down the left side of your neck right into your shoulder.

Hold for 25 seconds, then repeat with the right hand. Do this 3 times for each side.

Cervical Rotation

Turn your head left and look over your left shoulder stretching as far as possible.

Hold for 3 seconds, then turn the other way and hold for 3 seconds. Repeat 10 times each side.

Stretches designed to improve active range of motion can help alleviate headache symptoms.

FHA https://familyhealthadvocacy.com

TOP 7 NATURAL SOLUTIONS FOR HEADACHES OR MIGRAINES

TOP 7 NATURAL REMEDIES FOR HEADACHES OR MIGRAINES

7. Emotional Freedom Technique

This technique isn't just for headaches, it's been used to help with other body pains as well. The Emotional Freedom Technique is a natural treatment that has been used by practitioners for years. This is sometimes used as a back-up therapy when others have failed to exhibit positive or progressive results. This could be why it continues to grow in popularity with practitioners and patients alike.

As we have discussed in this report, there are many causes of headaches. Understanding the cause helps a health professional decide the course of care for correcting the problem. However sometimes pain relief is the only thing on your mind and correcting the cause may take time so some people come to rely on alternative modalities outside of taking medications. The Emotional Freedom Technique is one of those things to try. There are similarities to acupuncture however this technique is fantastic for those who don't like needles. This form of therapy doesn't inject any needles in the body, but involves tapping various pressure points all over the body. The goal of this therapy is to collect positive energy, raise energy levels, and then distributing them throughout the body. Practitioners of this technique liken it's affects to the blood flowing within the veins. A key ingredient to this technique is balance.

"
The Emotional Freedom Technique isn't just for headaches, it's been used to help with other body pains as well.
"

FHA   https://familyhealthadvocacy.com

COLIN SWALA

TOP 7 NATURAL SOLUTIONS FOR HEADACHES OR MIGRAINES

NATURAL REMEDIES FOR NUMBNESS AND TINGLING

7. Emotional Freedom Technique Cont...

This might sound really confusing but the technique works to sort emotions and physical balance. Even better, it's so simple that you can learn it and start to do it on yourself easily. However, it is recommended to start with a certified professional, especially where the situation is complex. There are some challenges doing the technique on yourself as preventative measures require very firm tapping and sometimes both sides of the body are tapped at the same time at a specified pace. Additionally, the tapping is done simultaneously with saying a phrase which allows the mind to be involved with positive affirmations. This is important to keep it from losing focus. The outcome... the level of pain is decreased and the intensity of your headache fades away slowly.

It's so simple that you can learn it and start to do it on yourself easily.

https://familyhealthadvocacy.com

162

Step 5: Create Your Warm Audience Facebook Ads Campaign.

It will take some time to build up the data from the cold audience, but in the meantime, let's get the warm audience Facebook ads campaign set up. When the timing is right we can then create the custom audience based on the data received from the cold audience interactions and launch these ads as follow up. Something that is important to understand is that your cold audience will be the largest, as you're only restricting the target to a specific location. Running the cold audience ads continuously should take the full year to run their course before ad fatigue fully takes effect. If you've developed 10 different topics with some extra variations in ad creative including videos and links, then that will be more than enough for Facebook to work its magic algorithm, showing the right ads at the right time to the right people. You should be monitoring the ads every couple of weeks to make sure that any ads aren't fatiguing, which also means the cost has gone up too high. When I started I made the mistake of thinking that Facebook marketing was like traditional marketing and that any one person needs to see a specific ad 4-6 times for it to be effective. It doesn't take long to discover that an ad with a frequency that high begins to underperform in Facebook. After asking a few reps at Facebook, the consensus seems to be that you'll want to make something new or shut off an ad after it hits the threshold of 3.

This point isn't as critical for the cold audience because, as I mentioned, it will be the biggest and therefore will take the longest to reach the frequency threshold. However, for this section we want to be able to create a custom audience based on interaction at the cold audience level, so the audience size will be smaller. Keep an eye on the frequency regularly. Never allow a frequency of 3 or higher to occur with any of the warm audience ads you run if your seeing your results taper at the same. By all means, if the frequency exceeds 3 and the results are maintaining then hold off but if a particular ad reaches that point, then it's time to shut it down and a new creative should take its place. You can recycle old ad creatives if you give ample time in between using them. Therefore, creating as many ad creatives as possible will help you in the long run.

Remember, it will take some time to fill this audience, so we can create the custom audience later after we have the data and choose the appropriate custom audience from the Ad set level of the campaign right before we activate it.

Lead Generation Facebook Ad for New Patient Appointment Opt-In

I absolutely love this Facebook ad campaign objective for generating new patient or client leads. You can quickly deliver the pertinent information about what they get if they opt-in for an appointment, and with a couple of clicks they can submit their contact information to you. Let's take a second to revise who these people are that will be seeing this ad. They have previously been exposed to loads of content that you've produced, they are starting to feel like they know and trust you, they may have seen some testimonials or have heard about success stories of other people in a similar position to them, and now they are waiting for instruction on how to take the next step. That's where these warm audience ads come in. This group of ads, the lead generation ads, are going to take them right to the option of sending you their information for an appointment. You can try to run these with no discount, which some health practitioners prefer to do, and you should have success if you've warmed them up enough. We have had the most success with providing a discount for the exam, which we sometimes combine with a date deadline.

Your ad creatives can be either a video or an image. Just make sure that you provide enough information in the text with an image that would compel these prospective patients or clients to take action. An interesting note is that we have predominantly been running video ads for our clients, as I heard that Facebook favors that form of media, but the image ad creative below has actually hit relevancy scores of 9 and 10!

For these types of ads you will need to create your form as well. You can really customize it to ask for any information you want, but we've included what we use in the examples below.

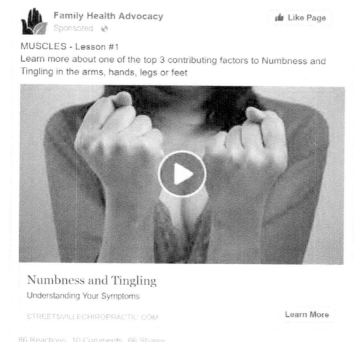

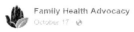

Family Health Advocacy
October 17

It's hard to be happy when every single day is endured with the complicated symptoms of numbness or tingling in the arms, legs, hands or feet. What makes it worse is that it's tough to find answers leaving no hope and being forced to just live with it.

There are many causes of these symptoms but the most that we've seen has been a combination of muscles, bones, joints and nerves which all play a vital role in these symptoms from cause to effect. Understanding the roles of each of these is where the answer can be found for most people.

It is not uncommon for patients to enter our office who have nerve disorders that are so severe that it causes them excruciating sharp, stabbing, and shooting pains that can radiate down their arms or legs, which can drastically alter their overall quality of life. So, if this is what is happening then you need help. There is not simple magic bullet solution for everyone.

Drs. Morgan and Casey Sinclair from Streetsville Chiropractic in Mississauga can help. Click "learn more" to find out how.

Numbness or Tingling
Doctors in Mississauga can help.

Learn More

👍 Like   💬 Comment   ↪ Share

Family Health Advocacy

Exam for only $40! (Normally $155)

- A thorough examination exploring all potential causes of your condition
- A complete neuromuscular examination
- Here's what you get:
- Specialized testing which may include x-rays if necessary
- A detailed plan of the course of action

Learn more by providing your info below.

What's the best time to contact you Monday-Friday?	Select ▾
Email	colin@trist.com
Full name	Colin Testy
Phone number	CA +1 ▾ 9054648556

By clicking Submit, you agree to send your info to Family Health Advocacy who agrees to use it according to their privacy policy. Facebook will also use it subject to our Data Policy, including to auto-fill forms for ads. View Facebook Data Policy. Family Health Advocacy Privacy Policy.

Conversions on Website/Landing Page

The next type of ad that we've seen work for both cold and warm audiences is creating a landing page. They can be basic with a video and opt-in form that is similar to the lead generation Facebook form yet more customizable. They can also be used to create an entire article on a topic to further educate, introduce yourself, and close with a call to action. We started our done-for-you service with these article types of landing pages, but I recommend that you trial both of them to see which work better in your location across various topics.

Here is an example of an article landing page. Notice that we've left the header of our website on the page, so it gives the feel of an article rather than a page where you're going to ask them for something:

BODY   MIND   NUTRITION   RECIPES   FAMILY HEALTH   WOMEN'S HEALTH   CHILDREN'S HEALTH   MEN'S HEALTH

If your life is afflicted by numbness or tingling in the arms, hands, fingers, legs, feet or toes then you will be interested in this clinical study that showed...

How Patients Significantly Improved Their Sharp Pains, Grip Strength, and Eliminated Numbness and Tingling Without Drugs or Surgery

Dr. Casey Sinclair, D.C.
Dr. Morgan Sinclair, D.C.
Streetsville Chiropractic

Special Ends Friday, December 1, 2017

Numbness, tingling, and pain affects all parts of your life

Numbness and tingling is a huge problem which affects every part of your life then sleeping, sitting or walking. The thought of getting a good night sleep or playing with your kids or grandchildren may seem like a pipe dream because your arms or legs are in too much pain and may even be weak.

Maybe you're frustrated because you've been told that you have to live with it as all the medical testing indicates that you shouldn't have a problem. Or maybe you're even fearful because the only options left are drugs with heavy side effects or surgery.

I can tell you one thing — you are not alone. Millions of people suffer from some form of peripheral neuropathy which can be caused by different things. It is described by science as a condition that results when nerves from the brain and spinal cord which carry messages to and from the rest of the body are damaged or disrupted.

This condition obstructs the nerve signals that control your muscles, joints, connective tissues and organs and if ignored could lead to more serious complications.

"I feel like I'm 30 years older than I actually am. I can't walk great distances without pain. My hands go numb while doing the simplest activities like watching tv or lying in bed. I am tired of living this way."

More Pills Are Not the Solution

We are Dr. Casey Sinclair and Dr. Morgan Sinclair from Streetsville Chiropractic in Mississauga. We have been helping people with nerve related conditions for over 6 years. We want to let you know that there is hope and you do have another option in Chiropractic that has been proven effective in removing pressure on the nerves without drugs or surgery.

There have been many clinical studies which have demonstrated the benefit of chiropractic and nerve conditions.

Patients showed an 85.5% resolution of the nerve symptoms after only 9 chiropractic treatments. - Journal of Chiropractic Medicine 2008

With chiropractic care, patients had "significant improvement in perceived comfort and function, nerve conduction and finger sensation overall." - JMPT 1998

"Significant increase in grip strength and improvement in motor and sensory latencies were noted. Orthopedic tests were negative. Symptoms dissolved." - JMPT 1994

Whilst these studies mean a lot there is hope for you to get your life back.

Where should you start?

Finding the cause of your neuropathy is where you start. The doctor of chiropractic is trained to identify the causes of neuromuscular conditions and if your case is beyond the scope of chiropractic you should be referred to the appropriate health professional. However, often these conditions are caused by a degeneration or misalignment of the spine which can press on the roots of the nerves. This pressure can arise from the bones or intervertebral discs anywhere on the spine from the base of the head down to the tail bone.

Whether you have been to a chiropractor before or this would be your first experience, you may be wondering what to expect with us. We want you to understand everything about your case and our procedures before we get started. Our exams are thorough and our patients describe our techniques as "gentle and effective". We have many techniques that we can use to ensure that you are comfortable without hindering the results of your care and progress.

The goal is to release pressure on the nerves to allow your body to heal.

Below is an example of a more basic landing page ad with a focus on video:

E-Report Download to Email Sequence

In the previous chapter on email marketing we gave an example of a landing page with an opt-in for an e-report followed by the 7-email sequence. In this chapter, we gave an example of the e-report to create and now it's time to tie all of that together. You can build the page on your website and connect it to your email marketing system or use a service like ClickFunnels to accomplish this. Here is a checklist of all the features and functionality that you'll need to have in place for this to work:

o   Generating traffic to the landing page either organically or paid
o   Landing page contains opt-in form
o   After successful opt-in, user is sent to confirmation page
o   Opt-in form connects with email marketing system adding subscribers to a list
o   Email Marketing System sends the download link via the automated 7-email sequence
o   Reports on email statistics

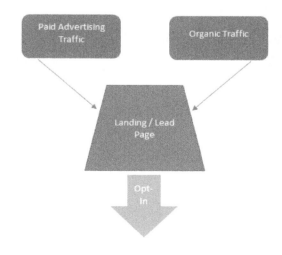

EMAIL MARKETING SYSTEM

Email #1 – Subject: _____

Email #2 – Subject: _____ Wait 1 day

Email #3 – Subject: _____ Wait 1 day

Email #4 – Subject: _____ Wait 1 day

Email #5 – Subject: _____ Wait 1 day

Email #6 – Subject: _____ Wait 2 days

Email #7 – Subject: _____ Wait 2 days

Confirmation Page – What Happens After They Opt-In?

Rather than simply displaying a message that their form has been submitted successfully, it's a valuable time to give them a little more and an immediate opportunity for an upsell. It's an appropriate time to first let them know about your special offer for an appointment. To continue with our examples, for people that opted in for the Numbness or Tingling E-report, we redirect them to a success page with more information and present "another FREE gift."

THE NEW PATIENT GENERATOR SETUP – DAY 13
(PAID SEARCH TRAFFIC – GOOGLE ADWORDS)

> *If it isn't on Google, it doesn't exist.*
> *– Jimmy Wales (Founder of Wikipedia)*

Harnessing the Power of Google Ads

You're probably aware that there are many search engines out there in internet land. It's by far the most widely used tool for searching the web. And if you've been on this planet long enough and had even the smallest bit of interest in computers, then you've probably heard of WebCrawler which was one of the first search engines widely used since the inception of the internet back in 1990. It was the first search engines that allowed you to search for any word in any webpage, which is basically how every search engine has worked since. However, the days of WebCrawler, AltaVista, and Yahoo leading the way are long gone and now Google is the king of the search engines in the online kingdom.

Harnessing the power of Google can be done two ways:

1) You can optimize your webpages so they rank higher in the search listings for specific keywords

2) You can pay to have your webpage links presented at the top
    of the list

Realistically, you'll be paying for both. Google's algorithms
are so complicated and take a lot of research and time to get
your pages ranking at the top. Time to learn this in addition
to digital marketing is probably something you don't have as a
health professional. We left this part out of this book because
just that topic alone deserves its own book. Most likely you'll
hire an expert to do that part for you anyway if that is the
route you want to go. Be prepared, however, because help
in that department can be expensive, maybe more expensive
than the second option which is the pay to play direction. It's
common, and I've made this mistake myself, to attempt to
use paid Google ads simply to get your website homepage link
to the top of the list for anyone searching a specific keyword
related to your practice. The hope is that they'll click, navigate
around on your website, discover from the piles of info you
have there that you can help them, and then pick up the phone
call you for an appointment. I've personally spent thousands
of dollars making this mistake. My ROI was basically negative
thousands of dollars.

For years following this marketing disaster I had a bad taste
in my mouth about Google AdWords. I fuelled my belief
that it wasn't effective by reading articles about the decline
in clicks for the ads across the platform, so I left it out of the
digital marketing equation. Then a few things hit me like a
bolt of lightening. Digital marketing can a numbers game
and it should be a safe strategy to hang around where the
majority of people are. I'm on Google searching at least 4 or
5 times per day, and clearly, I'm not alone as Google boasts
a whopping 3.5 billion searches worldwide per day. That's a
lot of eyes in one place. That was enough to peak my interest
again.

If you keep your Google Adwords account performance-based, which means your audience is paying per click rather than views, then the problem of the supposed decline in clicks through Google becomes less of a problem. If there's no traffic, then you don't pay. Nothing gained, nothing lost. If you are paying the same prices as the other paid advertising platforms per click then you've just opened up another door to meet your community from a different place for the same price.

In the last chapter, we discussed the 3 types of prospective patients or clients. Two of the three know that they have a problem and may be inclined to start taking action by searching on Google to learn more about it and what their options might be for help. This audience is different from Facebook, where the audience is not actively searching. The audience using Google search has intent. This gives you a distinct advantage with Google Ads, knowing that they've initiated their journey and just might be more inclined to receive whatever you're offering. By creating a Google AdWords campaign and running it alongside your Facebook initiatives you are maximizing your potential for new patient or client leads.

If you can remember all the way back to the chapter where we discussed brainstorming for trends that surround your industry, you can use the AdWords process to help reveal the most successful keywords. After running a variety of ads across hundreds of keywords around a condition or industry topic, you'll discover which ones covert prospective into actual patients or clients and then you can take that information back to your blog/article planning and ensure those keywords are included, therefore boosting your organic website traffic with higher search rankings.

For the purposes of this New Patient Generator system I will explain how to create Google Adwords that will send traffic to the 2 or 3 warm audience landing pages you created in the last few days from the previous chapter:

1) Basic Landing Page

2) Article Landing Page

3) E-report download Landing Page

Why are we sending what appears to be cold traffic to warm audience material? I have briefly mentioned earlier that there are a number of people that *are* ready to jump in at their first introduction anyway. However, in addition to that, when people go to Google, they're looking for something specific which means they're already a little warmer when compared to a cold Facebook audience. Save your marketing budget for sending people to blogs for Facebook and use Google primarily for your pages with a call to action.

Step 1: Ensure You Have a Google AdWords Account Setup.

If you own an android phone, then you probably already have a Gmail account, which is all you'll need to get started with Adwords. However, you may want to create a separate account for your practice. You can create a Google account with any address. You should have a website as well, but you can run ads without using Adwords Express.

The objective here is to create 2 Google ads for multiple keywords that surround the condition or topics you've chosen to move ahead with. You'll need to know how much you want to spend, what your target audience is, how you're going to bid for advertising space, what you want to say, and where you're going to send them when they click.

Step 2: Determine Your Maximum Cost Per Click, Then Choose The Audience and Bid Option.

Personally, for these types of ads I prefer to pay-per-click (CPC). This is what I recommend you select as your bidding option. These ads don't really incorporate much in the way of visual excitement like Facebook, so bidding for exposure or CPM doesn't really make sense to me for what we're trying to accomplish. I want to pay only when people end up on my landing pages and I don't want to overspend for the click. Depending on your market, if you don't cap what you're willing to pay for a click then I've heard of costs up to $100 per click but the good news is that for most topics relating to health practitioners you shouldn't have to pay more than $2.00, and I would probably set your cap at no more than $3.00 per click, but that really is up to you.

How much would you pay for a new patient request? I've seen services offering a pay-per-patient price of $120 and up. Although for many professions it goes against their regulatory body guidelines for marketing, it helps to determine what a typical going rate might be for a patient which you can use a baseline when reviewing your statistics. Realistically, you'll want to make sure that you're not spending more acquiring the patient than you'll receive from their care. One hundred and twenty dollars might sound expensive at first, but I would think that the total collections from a patient or client starting care with you should easily exceed that. Good news! You shouldn't be paying even close to that per request if you do this right. The better you get, the lower the cost per patient request you'll start to see.

For example, let's say that you would be happy paying $60 per patient or client. That means at your max bid of $3.00 (if you ever end up paying that) you would need to have your landing page convert 1 person for every 20 clicks, giving a conversion rate of 5 percent. That is a worst-case scenario as you could be paying as low as $0.50 per click which then you would need to convert 1 person for every 120 clicks, giving a conversion rate of 0.8 percent which should be very easy to achieve. The benchmark would be around a 5 percent conversion for new patient requests but can be anywhere from 1-5 percent. Good thing the cost per click is flexible which should balance everything out in the end. Conversions for e-reports we've seen much higher results hitting over 10 percent for some conditions or topics.

Step 3: Do Your Keyword Homework and Set Your Daily Budget.

Google has made it easy to split test your Google ads across many different keywords with the use of Ad Groups. With an idea of which keywords you'd like to target, the system will give you some suggested Ad Groups that contain anywhere between 50-100 related keyword combinations around your original suggestion which is very helpful. For the purposes of split testing, then I recommend using at least one Ad Group and monitoring the performance of each search term. Before activating the campaign, you can go through each Ad Group keyword list and modify any keywords that you would like to add or exclude. An important note is that you want to keep the keywords that have a high intent versus those with low intent. These keywords are considered to have high commercial intent meaning they have strong intent for a user to conduct an action, like requesting an appointment with you for example.

When setting up your ad you'll first be given the option to choose between the following:

- Search Network
- Display Network
- Shopping
- Video

- Universal App

I'm not going to go into detail about each of these, but my recommendation is to start with the Search Network only. This will be the most effective for your new patient or client goals because these are the ads that are displayed on the Google search engine results page, the place where the prospective patients or clients are most ready to take the next step if they discover something of interest. For our purposes, this is more effective than the Display Network, which shows ads across a network of websites on relevant pages. This displays your ad to people not specifically searching for it, which isn't a bad thing, however, we're already using Facebook to accomplish that because it works better.

Step 4: Create Your Ads.

Consider for a moment how your ads are displayed on Facebook and what they look like. They are media-rich, including images, slideshows, and videos. You have plenty of opportunity to ad flare and draw attention even if your ad copy (Copywriting is the act of writing text for the purpose of advertising or other forms of marketing) isn't very stellar. Now picture the Google search results page. What's there? Almost nothing but text. Do you think it's possible that it may be harder to stand out in the crowd on there? Absolutely. A good place to start is to try some searches of your own and see what stands out. You don't need to reinvent the wheel. Just have a look to see what catches your eye and roll with it. It's not a good idea, however, to completely copy someone else's idea, especially if you're targeting the same keywords.

I've seen some practices that have paid for Google ads and simply displayed their practice information as the text. I see the logic here as it puts your brand at the top of the search. Hooray! However, if someone searches for neck pain, and that particular practice's paid ad was displayed at the top with a headline "John's Acupuncture Clinic – Get help today" and the next paid ad down has the headline "Free Download" – Natural Solutions for Neck Pain" which do you think is going to get the click? You need to have some type of eye-catching call to action to entice the audience to click through to your page.

Another little tip is you want to make your text as relevant to what the person searched as possible. Notice in the 2 examples I mentioned in the previous paragraph, the first didn't include the searched keyword while the second one did. If someone is searching neck pain, I'll be pretty sure that they're scouring the results page for the words "neck" and "pain" so that's a great way to stand out. Google even allows you to make headlines by subbing in what the searcher has typed. You can use the following code to replace your headline or a portion of it with whatever the searcher types:

{Keyword: *Default Headline*}

Simply replace the part that is italicized with whatever you want your default to be. Google will try to replace the portion of the headline with the closest keyword to what the user typed, and if not possible, then it will use what you typed here. That's actually quite amazing!

Here are some examples of Google Ads that we made to send traffic to the free numbness and tingling e-report download landing page:

FREE {keyword: Trapped Nerve} Report - Top 9 Natural Solutions

[Ad] familyhealthadvocacy.com/free-report/trapped-nerve

Limited Time Only! Learn How to Heal Numbness or Tingling Naturally

Example ad

With this example, we saw a click through rate of 10 percent which is way above normal. The average is 2 percent so anything above that then you should feel confident that your ad is performing well. Remember you are going to want to create ads for all the landing pages you created; the e-report download, the landing page with the new patient request form, and the article page with the new patient request form.

THE NEW PATIENT GENERATOR SETUP – DAY 14
(ANALYTICS)

"Data! Data! Data! I can't make bricks without clay!"
– Sir Arthur Conan Doyle

Boring but Necessary

Throughout this book I've given many digital marketing ideas and examples, and there's a good chance that if you simply copy what I've presented, with minor tweaks to make them applicable to your industry, the system would be successful. However, could it be better? Absolutely. That's why understanding how to analyze the results from your digital marketing initiatives is essential. Essential for optimization. Essential for proving the return on investment (ROI) of your digital marketing initiatives. Each month you should be reviewing the statistics and trying new things to improve your results and making sure that you are at least seeing a positive ROI. However, it's easier said than done because it's boring and challenging. What I'm asking you to do here is to analyze both your web analytics (traffic, bounce rate, unique visitors, or average time on page) and the analytics from your advertising platforms.

By now I would hope that you know that digital marketing goes well beyond the confines of your website. We also need to know about all the origins of the traffic, the effectiveness of each individual ad initiative, number of leads for each, number of actual live patients or clients from each initiative, and the collections received from those patients or clients. With that information you can direct more of your marketing budget towards what's working rather than wasting money on what isn't. You can compare how well your organic web traffic stands up against your paid social media initiatives. You can see differences in your conversion rates between taking your audience through a journey of cold and warm ad creatives before asking for action versus simply asking right off the hop. One of the most important things I've learned is that there is not a "one size fits all" solution for digital marketing, and the only way to really optimize your digital marketing initiatives is to understand the metrics, and based on them, know what actions to take.

In this section we will be covering the most important metrics for Facebook, Google AdWords, Google Analytics (for your blogs, webpages or landing pages), and your email marketing.

Facebook Metrics

I've written pages of information in this book about how to set up your Facebook ads and some tips to get started optimizing them. But if you really want to keep the new patient generating machine oiled up, then you must be able to effectively gauge performance and customize. I don't like wasting money and I'll go out on a limb to say that you probably don't as well. If you don't enjoy analytics then I'm sorry to say, you're going to have to look beyond the number of "likes" you get or how many people you've "reached" to measure the success of your Facebook ads and ultimately receive better value for your money spent. The good news is, however, I'm going to keep this as simple as possible because it's one of those "how far down the rabbit hole do you want to go" scenarios. You can get most of the information you need to make decisions from the following Facebook ad metrics.

- CLICK THROUGH RATE (ALL VERSUS LINK) – These are solid metrics to analyze how much your audience is interacting with your ad. There are two click through rate (CTR) metrics to view. CTR "all" and CTR "links." CTR "links" refers to the percentage of people that your ad was shown to that specifically clicked anything connected to a link or call-to-action (CTA) button. Whereas CTR "all" includes any link or CTA button clicks but also anything else clickable like a "like" or "reaction" icon, expanding text to read more, or even clicking to comment or share. Both metrics have value and obviously CTR "all" will always be higher because it includes CTR "links" as well. Generally, the higher the interaction with your ad, the more Facebook will show the ad to your audience for your set budget. This would normally translate into more new patient or client leads. If you're split testing many ad creatives, then after about a week or two, you can use this metric with the others from this section to drop the weakest ones.

> According to wordstream.com, the average click through rate (CTR) is 0.84 percent for the healthcare industry. The good news is that if you follow the directions from this book then you will be averaging much higher than that. You want to shoot for 5-7 percent, and although you'll probably average 2-3 percent, it's good to set the bar high. It's important to note that even the best ads will start strong and then slowly fatigue over time as the frequency numbers rise (see Frequency metric below). So you'll have to set a schedule and monitor these metrics regularly.

- RELEVANCE SCORE – Some digital marketing experts will tell you to ignore this metric. I'm going to say ignore these digital marketing experts on this advice. However, I will agree that you shouldn't make your decisions based on this metric alone. If you have an ad with a low relevance score that generated 10 new patient or client requests in a week, then you probably want to keep that creative going. Their argument is that since this is a possibility then the metric should be ignored. However, I've experienced that scenario to be the minor exception and not the rule. Low relevancy equals less reach for your daily budget, which generally produces less new patient or client leads which is our main goal for generating new patient interest. The metric is a scale from 1-10 with 10 being the best. The score is generally determined by the feedback from the audience interactions with your ad. Also, this metric only applies to some of the ad objectives. If you are running video views, conversions, or leads then the relevance metric is applicable for your campaign. performance. However, if you're running an awareness campaign like ads bought through reach and frequency, then this metric doesn't apply.

- CONVERSIONS / LEADS – This metric is one of the most important measurements of your campaign success. This refers to the total number of conversions or leads you've received. Note that conversion and leads are separate metrics and you will be referring to the one you've selected as your campaign objective. This reflects the total number of new patient or client requests your campaigns have produced or also actions like opting in to receive your free e-book or reports or whichever lead magnet you've offered. This is a great metric to use for goal setting and should be noted on a stats sheet. For example, if you set a goal of 20 new patient requests in a month, then you can use this metric to check your results.

- COST PER ACTION (CONVERSION/LEAD) – This metric will help you determine your return-on-investment. Your CPA is detailing exactly how much you're spending with Facebook to produce each action whether it's an opt-in for download or a new patient or client request. You should also be tracking the number of patients or clients that arrive in your practice. Noting those that start care, and together with your average collections for each new patient or client, then you can determine the real breakeven point for your campaigns. The average CPA will be much different depending on the action your tracking or the industry that you're in.

- FREQUENCY – This is probably the most important metric for determining why a solid ad creative's performance declines over time. Ads do have a shelf life. If you have a large audience, say the size of a whole country, state, or province, then the shelf life will be longer than if you are in a small town of ten thousand people. As I mentioned earlier in this book, when I started using Facebook ads years ago I made the mistake of thinking that the old marketing research applies that states that an individual should see an ad like 5 or 6 times before it becomes effective. So that was the goal. It didn't take too long to discover that the performance of every ad started to decline when the frequency number reached somewhere between 2 and 3. To be safe, now we will completely change up the ad creative when a particular ad reaches that number unless it is still producing the desired number of leads or conversions.

- COST PER CLICK (CPC)/COST PER THOUSAND IMPRESSIONS (CPM) – Although the CPA is probably the best metric for understanding if the entire Facebook campaign initiative is worth doing in the first place, you can use CPC and CPM to determine if you're overspending for your ad exposure. According to wordstream.com, the average CPC for the healthcare industry is $1.32 so that should be used as your benchmark and you should aim for a CPM under $10.

- AMOUNT SPENT – This is self-explanatory. When calculating your ROI you will want to know the total amount spent for your campaigns.

- VIDEO VIEWS – One of three metrics for your campaigns that include video, although probably the least important to use in your ad performance evaluations. If you're running a video views objective to a cold audience for the sole purpose of educating the public, then you may be interested in the total number of views a particular video has received. However, the metric doesn't give you any information about how much of the video has been watched. I think that is a more valuable metric. This one, however, could be used for boasting if ever the need to. "Over 1 million views worldwide! Be sure to share this viral video with your friends and family."

- AVERAGE VIDEO VIEW PERCENTAGE – This will show you the average amount of your video that is watched by the people who viewed it. If you have a video packed with information, then your goal will be to have as many people as possible watch the video for as long as possible. You can use this metric to compare audience interest. Making a strong first impression with your video is crucial, and if the first 10 seconds can evoke interest and emotion, then the more likely the viewer will want to continue watching. You can create a few different videos with various intro creatives and compare results.

- VIDEO VIEWS BY PERCENTAGE – Very useful to know. As with the average video view percentage, your goal is to increase the numbers of people watching higher percentages of the full video. Where these also come in handy is when you're going to start retargeting the people who watched the video. You know that people who have watched the video 75 percent or higher are going to be hotter than those who watched 10 percent of the video. That way you can develop retargeting that is applicable to each group.

Google AdWords Metrics

If you haven't been killed by boredom from the last section, then let's keep pushing on. Understanding all these metrics can be overwhelming as there are dozens of ways to present the data and many naming conventions that in most cases are measuring the same things. The good news is that most of what you just learned in the previous section can be applied here. Analysis of your AdWords performance is also done but looking at metrics like:

- Cost per conversion – Average cost to get each conversion
- Click Through Ratio – How often the ad was clicked when it was displayed
- Cost per click – Average cost per click based on number of clicks divided by total amount spent
- Conversion Rate – How often clicks resulted in conversions
- Quality Score – The rating of quality and relevance of both your keywords and PPC ads

Just like with Facebook, your goal is to optimize your campaigns by spending your marketing dollars on what's working and dropping what isn't. The goal is the same. You want more of the keywords and ads that result in new patient or client requests or more opt-ins to your mailing list. The simple rule to follow is that you want to keep the ads that are converting and then within that group you want to keep the keywords that are providing you a lower cost per conversion.

Also, make sure you take advantage of the charts available for the metrics listed above. The tables are great but where they lack is the ability to effectively show performance over a given time period. You will have to select various time periods and compare the numbers to get this information from the table; however, the chart can show it all in one pop. This is also a useful tip for Facebook Ad metric analysis as well.

Google Analytics (GA) Metrics

Most the features provided by Google Analytics are useful for search engine optimization (SEO) for the webpages on your website, which we haven't covered in this book as that topic as well deserves its own book. However, because we've talked about blogging, you should know about these metrics that will help you optimize the traffic to these pages:

- SESSIONS AND USERS – Formally known as "visits" and "unique visitors," these metrics allow you to track the popularity of a given page. The old terminology didn't need explaining as the names explained themselves, but now you will have to keep a mental note that sessions refers to the total number of hits or visitors for a given page and Users refers to the unique number of people visiting a given page.

- DEMOGRAPHICS, LANGUAGES, AND LOCATION – You can access complete age, gender, language preference, and location reports. You should be tracking organic conversions as well and you will need Google Analytics set up for that. Much like Google AdWords, you will be able to find out which groups are most likely to convert.

- BOUNCE RATE – Considered to be one of the most misunderstood GA metrics. This DOES NOT report on how quick a visitor leaves your website or page. This DOES measure a percentage of people that enter onto a page versus the number of times they leave. A page that has all visitors arrive and then leave the whole website without clicking onward within the site would be given a 100 percent bounce rate. This is important when trying to improve your visitor experience, which is something that Google takes into consideration when ranking pages on their search engine. High bounce rates can be an indication of how irrelevant your page is for a given topic, so paying attention to internal navigation to keep them on site checking out related links or articles will help reduce that number.

- AVERAGE TIME ON PAGE – This is an important measurement that is believed to play a part in search engine optimization. A common theme that you may have picked up in this book is that many of these web platforms have a goal to continue to improve the user experience, and content that achieves that is rewarded whether the ads are cheaper, or pages are organically ranked higher. This metric is a way to know if visitors are actually reading your content. If the average time spent on the page is only 5 seconds, then it's pretty obvious they're not reading. You may have come across these blogs that are so detailed and go on forever full of valuable information? That's because the longer they can keep more people engaged, the more credible that page will be considered for the topic it covers, and Google will rank the page higher in the search.

- TRAFFIC SOURCES – Keeping track of where the traffic from your blogs or landing pages is coming from is essential. Even more important is to know which sources are converting for the lowest cost. In this book we've had you create blog articles purely for information, blog articles that have a call-to-action like requesting a new patient or client appointment, or simple landing pages with email opt-ins for free downloads. How are people finding their way to these pages? Do some sources of traffic convert more than others? Do some convert cheaper than others? With this information you can better allocate your budget to improve results.

- INBOUND LINKS – Another search engine rank booster for a page is to have as many links to it from other pages out on the web. The more credible the website linking to you, the more link "juice" it's worth. In a perfect world your pages would be filled with so much valuable information that people everywhere making webpages around your topic would find your page and link to you without you having to lift a finger. The world has a long way to go to be perfect, so my advice is to not wait for that to happen and take initiative to promote your pages by connecting with people and try to have them to link to you. Whether it just happens naturally, or you've earned your link "juice," you can use this metric to see where all the backlinks are coming from for your pages.

Email Marketing Metrics

In this book I gave you a basic starting ground to email marketing. Whole books, however, are written on how to perfect it and expand the campaigns to fill a calendar year. When it comes down it, however, it doesn't matter how many tips you learn because if you can't comprehend or even view your results you won't be progressing. You need to know exactly what your goal is and the metrics to track to ensure you're progressing in the desired direction. Depending on which email marketing platform you choose will determine how much analysis you can perform. As much as I love how easy Aweber is to use, the performance metrics for the campaigns are not quite there yet. To properly analyze email marketing success, you'll need a platform that will give you the following data:

- OPEN RATE – First in line for email marketing metrics. You aren't going to progress your emailing audience through their journey if they're not even opening the emails. A poor open rate could mean you need a more compelling subject line.

- CLICK THROUGH RATE (CTR) – Just like your paid Facebook and Google Ads, the primary goal is to drive traffic to your blogs or landing pages for further engagement, education, or action. If you have a high open rate with a poor CTR then your email content is not enticing enough to progress your reader to the next step. You must summon the click!

- CONVERSION RATE – If you've managed to peak the interest of your subscriber enough that they open your email, they read the content and want more so they clicked your link and ended up on your landing page, this metric will be the percentage of subscribers that follow through with the desired action on that page. For example, someone requesting a new patient or client appointment.

- BOUNCE RATE – Much different than the bounce rate I mentioned with the tracking of webpages in Google Analytics. This metric measures the deliverability of your emails. If anyone on your list has an incorrect or false address, then emails will be undeliverable. If the bounce rate goes too high, then some email marketing providers might terminate your service so be careful and keep your lists clean. You can check how clean your lists are by exporting them and checking them with services like https://neverbounce.com.

- LIST GROWTH RATE – This will help you track how successful your list building campaigns are doing. Tracking unsubscribes is key here has well. If you have a high unsubscribe rate then you should double check how you are acquiring subscribers, how you're explaining your intentions, and what content your providing. If the whole process isn't connecting or congruent then you will probably see many subscribers dropping off.

- SOCIAL SHARING OR EMAIL FORWARDING – Taking note of how many forwards or shares with social media a particular email gets is probably one of the most important indicators for the quality of an email. With conversion as the main objective with your emails, they only go out to people on your list. If emails get shared or forward to others, then you've just opened up an opportunity to grow your list even further. Optimizing your emails should include forwarding and social sharing in addition to link clicks. Keep an eye on which content gets shared the most as you could then develop more of what they love.

Step 1: Set Up Your Google Analytics Account.

You've got a website, you've written blogs or articles, but how many people are visiting the pages? Are they actually reading the articles? How long are they spending on the pages or your site? What are the most popular channels for them to find your content? That's where Google Analytics comes in, but you can't reap the benefits until you have it properly installed and set up.

a) Create a Google Analytics account – Go to https://www.google.com/analytics/ and sign in with the account you created from Google AdWords implementation section. Input your account name, name your website and add the website URL (address), choose your industry category and time zone. Choosing the correct industry category enables Google Analytics to open access to industry related benchmark stats.

b) Add the code to your website – Adding the tracking code

to the right place on your website correctly is essential for the service to work. If you have a web person, then they can help you with this part. You'll need to copy the code from the Website Tracking section anyway and either email to your web person to implement or follow the instructions provided to install. Most of the big web platforms like WordPress have a field where you can copy the code or Google Analytics ID to make it easy for you.

c) Test the installation – Now it's time to ensure your website and pages are actually sending data to Google Analytics. Simply go and navigate around on the pages of your website and then open a new window in your browser and go to your Google Analytics account. Navigate to the Real-Time section, which should show your activity on the site.

d) Share access to the data (if necessary) – It's possible that you will be too busy with all the other duties of running a busy practice, so you'll probably want to delegate the job of collecting data to someone else. To grant access, go to the admin section and choose User Management. You can select the level of access you wish to allow the user and simply add their email address and click save. The user must have a Google account already in the system for this to work.

Step 2: Create Your Analytics Master Tracking Sheet.

Due to the overwhelming amount of digital marketing data from multiple sources, it will be much easier for you and your team to analyze and make decisions if all the key performance indicators (KPI) were consolidated into one place. That's why I suggest you create a master tracking sheet that is updated bi-weekly or monthly and brought to your team meetings in order to keep your new patient generating machine greased up. You should include a section for every digital marketing element you've implemented, their corresponding KPIs, and compare over time.

For example:

INITIATIVES	DATE			
Facebook Personal Profile Posts	**Friends**	**Reactions**	**Shares**	**Comments**
Post 1 "Description"				
Post 2 "Description"				
...				
Facebook Practice Page Posts	**Reach/Views**	**Reactions**	**Shares**	**Comments**
Post 1 "Description"				
Post 2 "Description"				
...				
Facebook Practice Page	**Followers**	**Reach**	**Engagement**	**Neg. Feedback**
Pages Insights				
YouTube Videos	**Views**	**Drop-off**	**Likes**	**Dislikes**
Video 1 "Description"				
...				
Instagram Stories	**Unique Views**	**Number at 1st**	**Number at last**	**Completion Rate = (# at 1st / # at last) x 100**
Instagram Story 1 "Description"				

...				
Twitter Tweets	**Impressions**	**Link Clicks**	**Likes**	**Retweets**
Tweet 1 "Description"				
Tweet 2 "Description"				
...				
Email Campaign	**Open Rate**	**CTR**	**Bounce**	**Social**
Email 1 "Description"				
Email 2 "Description"				
...				
Blogs	**Users**	**Avg. Time on Page**	**Top Traffic Source**	**# of Inbound Links**
Blog/Article 1 "Description"				
Blog/Article 2 "Description"				
...				

PAID INITIATIVES	DATE			
Facebook Cold Audience Ads	Conversion / Leads	Cost Per Action	Frequency	CTR
Ad 1 "Description"				
Ad 2 "Description"				
...				
Facebook Warm Audience Ads	Conversion / Leads	Cost Per Action	Frequency	CTR
Ad 1 "Description"				
Ad 2 "Description"				
...				
Google AdWords	Cost Per Conversion	Cost per Click	Conv. Rate	CTR
Ad 1 "Description"				
Ad 2 "Description"				
Ad 3 "Description"				

Simply collecting the data isn't enough. If you're not under-standing the data and making changes based on your findings, then it becomes just some fun "water cooler" talk. You will be able to track trends and adjust your campaigns to deliver more of what is working and at the same time be trying out new ideas. Debatably quoted by Einstein and one of the most overused quotes going, "The definition of insanity is doing the same thing over and over and expecting a different result." Get your results, read your results, and take action based on your results.

EPILOGUE

*"If you do not change direction, you may end up
where you are heading." – Lao Tzu*

Pop the Champagne!

Congratulations! By now you should have completed the
construction of your new patient generating machine. This
achievement is not for the lazy, that's for sure, but when has lazi-
ness ever offered you anything exceptional in return? The moment
I decided that I wanted to write a book on the subject, I realized
that there were two directions that I could go. I could've written
a digital marketing book of stories boasting all the successes we've
had with clients over the years, which I understand may have been
both entertaining and a credibility builder. However, I thought
to myself that a practical step-by-step guide is something that I
would find more useful, so why wouldn't everyone else? I realize
that most of this book is technical mumbo jumbo, but I really
wanted to deliver a complete schematic to the machine that,
once built, would actually be a game changer for your practice
like it was for mine and many others. The 14 days of hard work
should set the framework for a career-long digital marketing
endeavour that will provide an evergreen pathway for people in
your community to find their way into your practice. Only a very
small percentage of your colleagues would have accomplished
what you have because it's not easy and takes hard work and
dedication. However, as the world continues to shift into a

digital space you made the smart decision to ride the wave like a pro surfer rather than have the wave crush and drown you like a poser as others ride ahead.

I feel truly grateful for this opportunity to share this knowledge with you. Any effort towards creating more automation in business I think is worth every second. It allows you to have more fun in practice as it offers you more time to focus mentally on your patients or clients care rather than where they will be coming from next. Your practice's patient or client base continues to grow exponentially as a result which decreases financial burden. You can then afford to allocate more time to your health and family. This is an exciting cascade that all can result from the work you and your team have put into this.

Maintenance on Your Machine

Just like regular maintenance on your car, the new patient generating machine that you built will require maintenance as well. The good news is that you have the framework and schedule, so now it's just about keeping up with current content and creatives for your ads. The machine was built to spread your message to as many people in your community as possible, on regular basis, who continually feel they are receiving value, look to you as the expert in your field, and trust that you have the solutions to their health challenges. Over time, what your audience values will change and what interests them will change. If you don't stay on top of that then your new patient engine will break down. Fortunately, we've given you the tips on how to stay current and relevant so use the tools outlined in this book to guide you. As a rule of thumb, you can't go wrong if you are consistently delivering something that is helpful, versus always trying to sell. The sales will naturally follow the valued help.

Use this checklist to make sure you've implemented all the elements discussed in this book. Play around. Test ads from your warm audience with your cold audience. As much as we've given you a framework here, the more you test, the better you will understand ad performance for your industry and your location.

IMPLEMENATION SCHEDULE DAY 1 - 14

DAY 1

o Determine Your Blog Platforms
o Write 2 Blogs

DAY 2

o Write 2 Blogs

DAY 3

o Write 2 Blogs
o Create Twitter Account
o Research Relevant Twitter Chats
o Create YouTube Account
o Create Instagram Account
o Create Facebook Personal Facebook Page
o Create Facebook Practice Page
o Create 4 Patient or Client Avatars
o Create 10 Personal Profile Posts

DAY 4

- o Write 2 Blogs
- o Write 15 Tweets
- o Write 3 Video Scripts
- o Choose Instagram Story Day of the Week
- o Create 10 Personal Profile Posts
- o Create 20 Personal Practice Page Posts
- o Engage 5x on social media (Groups, Twitter chats, Pages, etc.)

DAY 5

- o Write 2 Blogs
- o Write 15 Tweets
- o Write 3 Video Scripts
- o Develop format for weekly Instagram story
- o Create 10 Personal Profile Posts
- o Create 10 Personal Practice Page Posts
- o Engage 5x on social media (Groups, Twitter chats, Pages, etc.)
- o Create Your Facebook Group(s)

DAY 6

- o Record 1 video and publish
- o Setup your customer/client review profiles

DAY 7

---

o Record 1 video and publish
o Choose your email marketing system
o Obtain 1 patient/client online review

DAY 8

---

o Record 1 video and publish
o Write 7 email sequence and set up email automation
o Obtain 1 patient/client online review

DAY 9

---

o Record 1 video and publish
o Map out the annual events for email broadcasting
o Obtain 1 patient/client online review

DAY 10

---

o Develop up to 10 cold audience Facebook Ads
o Record 1 video and publish
o Obtain 1 patient/client online review

DAY 11

- o Develop your lead magnet
- o Record 1 video and publish
- o Obtain 1 patient/client online review

DAY 12

- o Develop up to 3 warm audience Facebook Ads
- o Obtain 1 patient/client online review

DAY 13

- o Develop 2 warm audience style Google AdWords ads
- o Obtain 2 patient/client online reviews

DAY 14

- o Setup Google Analytics account
- o Develop your digital marketing master tracking sheet

MAINTENANCE (DAILY)

o Engage on Facebook (Pages or Groups), Twitter, Instagram, YouTube or Blogs
o Engage in your personal Facebook group

MAINTENANCE (WEEKLY)

o Write 1 video script, record and publish
o Develop a new Instagram story
o Engage in Twitter Chats
o Obtain 1 patient/client online review
o 3-5 New Facebook posts to your practice page
o 7-10 New Tweets

MAINTENANCE (MONTHLY)

o Update digital marketing master tracking sheet
o Plan topics for upcoming month based on stats from tracking sheet
o Update segmentation of email lists (active/inactive/prospective)

MAINTENANCE (ANNUAL)

o   Revise patient / client avatars
o   Develop your annual email broadcast campaign schedule
o   Develop emails for your broadcasts
o   Review digital marketing master tracking sheet and set goals

Signing Off

This has been a blast writing this book and I hope that you feel that it was worth exploring. I wish you all the best on your journey forward, and I hope that the tools provided in this book will allow you to further your prosperity. Furthermore, I anticipate that those in your community that were falling short looking for solutions to their health challenges will finally find their answers.

Made in the USA
Monee, IL
26 May 2021